Glass
of the '20s & '30s

A Collector's Guide

Glass
of the '20s & '30s
A Collector's Guide

Frankie Leibe

Special Consultant:
Jeanette Hayhurst

MILLER'S

MILLER'S GLASS OF THE '20S & '30S: A COLLECTOR'S GUIDE
by Frankie Leibe
Special consultant: Jeanette Hayhurst

First published in Great Britain in 1999 by Miller's, a division of
Mitchell Beazley, imprints of Octopus Publishing Group Ltd,
Michelin House, 81 Fulham Road, London SW3 6RB

Miller's is a registered trademark of Octopus Publishing Group Ltd

Executive Editor **Alison Starling**
Executive Art Editor **Vivienne Brar**
Project Editor **Elisabeth Faber**
Assistant Editor **Clare Peel**
Designers **Louise Griffiths & Adrian Morris**
Illustrator **Amanda Patton**
Indexer **Sue Farr**
Production **Rachel Staveley**
Specially commissioned photography by **Premier Photography**
Jacket photography by **Steve Tanner**

The publishers will be grateful for any information that will assist them
in keeping future editions up to date. Although all reasonable care has
been taken in the preparation of this book, neither the publishers nor
the compilers can accept any liability for any consequence arising from
the use thereof, or the information contained therein.

ISBN 1 84000 070 8
A CIP catalogue record for this book is available from the British Library
Set in Bembo, Frutiger and Shannon
Colour reproduction by Vimnice Printing Press Co. Ltd., Hong Kong
Produced by Toppan Printing Co., (HK) Ltd.
Printed and bound in China

Jacket (left to right): champagne/cocktail glass by Daum, 1930s; trailed vase
by Whitefriars, 1935; engraved vase by Walsh, 1930s; moulded opalescent
vase by Jobling, c.1934; "rainbow" posy vase by Royal Brierley, 1930s

contents

Where to start

Trends in collecting glass tend to be some five years behind those in ceramics, so, although the ceramics of the 1920s and 1930s were being rediscovered in the late 1960s and early 1970s, it was not until the mid- to late-1970s that the glass of the inter-war years began to be explored. What collectors discovered was a wide range of glass, much of it in traditional and historical styles, together with pieces by designers who used and revived traditional glassmaking techniques such as acid-etching, enamelling, *pâte-de-verre*, moulding, and pressing to create the new Art Deco styles and motifs inspired by an era of hedonism, glamour, speed, and travel.

This book is a good, accessible introduction to the glass that was produced in quantity throughout Europe, Scandinavia, and the USA in the 1920s and 1930s. As a novice collector, you can use it to gain a broad overview of the subject, perhaps before trying to narrow the field by focusing on a particular collecting theme such as technique, type, country, factory, style – whether traditional, historical, or Art Deco, or that of a particular designer – that you can explore in more depth with the help of the books listed in *What to read* (see pp.62–3).

Unmarked and unattributed glass is modestly priced and readily available, but if your first piece can be attributed to either a factory or a designer, this will provide a starting-point from which you can build up

your knowledge by reading in your local library, researching in museums, visiting vetted fairs, and, above all, handling glass. A reputable dealer is an essential part of this process. He or she can supply information, answer questions, provide an opportunity to handle pieces, and – most importantly – build up a good long-term relationship that is mutually beneficial. Do not feel that you have to buy every time you visit; never be afraid to ask the price, and do not be afraid to say if you cannot afford a piece – many dealers take credit cards or are prepared to make arrangements for payments in stages. Do buy what you like and the very best you can afford. A £50 piece once a month may well become a £100 piece every two months, as your knowledge and tastes develop.

As your collection grows (as it inevitably will) you will need to decide how to show it off. A display cabinet (especially one that is Art Deco in style) is ideal and solves the problem of dusting; glass shelving in alcoves with down lighting is an alternative, but pieces will need to be cleaned with an anti-static duster; frosted bathroom windows can often provide a perfect background for transparent coloured glass. If you are displaying heavy items, 8mm (⅓in) or 10mm (⅜in) shelves will be needed rather than the standard 6mm (¼in). Pieces that are not on display should be stored in bubble wrap or newspaper in a cool dry place; warmth and damp are a dangerous combination when storing glass, as print from damp newspaper will transfer to the surface of the glass. Glass can withstand extremes of temperature but not sudden changes of heat. Wash pieces in tepid soapy water, or clean with a spray-on glass cleaner, and finish with a paper kitchen towel. Dishwashers and glass are not compatible; the water is far too hot and bakes any limescale onto the surface of the glass.

Vulnerability will be an important consideration, as glass is very easy to break. A compromise on insurance is a false economy, so if possible insure your collection separately. Photograph your pieces and keep detailed records of what you bought, the place and date of purchase, the price paid and condition each piece was in, together with the descriptive receipts that a good dealer will provide.

Good condition is most important. Check for damage or restoration by feeling, looking, and asking. If a perfect example of a particular technique or form is outside your price range, a damaged affordable piece may be better than no example at all and will certainly be a useful learning aid. Prices for glass vary greatly, but, apart from such notable exceptions as pieces by Lalique or Gallé, in general 1920s and 1930s glass is modestly priced, it is important to remember that a piece does not have to be highly priced to be good. Buy what you like, buy the best example you can afford, and if and when you no longer like it, sell it and trade up. Never abandon hope – if the piece you set your heart on has been sold, you were probably not meant to have it in the first place. The agonies you experience over the pieces you cannot buy will soon be replaced by the ecstasies you feel over the pieces you can.

Prices and dimensions

Prices for antiques vary, depending on the condition of the item, geographical location, and market trends, so the price ranges given throughout this book should be seen as guides to value only.

Abbreviations used for dimensions are as follows: **ht** height; **diam.** diameter; **l.** length. Dimensions are given in both centimetres and inches.

Blown glass

Blowing is one of the earliest and simplest glassmaking techniques. The glassblower collects a gather of molten glass on the end of the blowing iron and blows it to the desired size by either free-blowing or blowing into a mould, continuously spinning the glass to create an even surface. The glass is then transferred to a solid rod, known as a "pontil iron", for shaping. When the required shape and size are achieved, the piece is removed from the rod and allowed to cool slowly. In the 1920s and 1930s the technique was an integral part of the return to good simple form that was a basic tenet of the Modernist architects. Swedish glassmakers and such architect-designers as British-based Keith Murray used the malleable nature of glass to produce bold, contemporary shapes that are now highly collectable.

▼ Vase by Murray

New Zealand-born architect Keith Murray was employed from 1932 as a freelance designer at the firm of Stevens & Williams, of Brierley Hill, near Stourbridge. The bold modern form of this simple free-blown vase with a rim flared with tools clearly shows the influence of Murray's architectural training. Overall symmetry, a smooth surface, and impeccable blowing are all essential with such minimalist pieces, which are increasingly sought after.

Although marks are often difficult to decipher, this vase is acid-etched with the "Keith Murray" signature and the words "Royal Brierley".

Vase by Murray, 1930s, ht 19cm/7in, **£200–300**

▶ Vase by Murray

This large free-blown pale blue vase, also designed by Murray, features spotted decoration created by small pockets of air. The gather of glass was slightly expanded by blowing and then dipped into a mould with indentations; it was cooled slightly before being covered with another layer of hot glass, which because of the temperature difference did not flow into the indentations. The Keith Murray mark on the base is very indistinct, but the form is clearly identified as number 307A in the catalogue of Murray patterns.

Vase by Murray, 1934/5, ht 31cm/12in, **£350–450**

Ice-glass bowl, 1920s,
ht 7.5cm/3in, £40–60

Vase by Orrefors, 1932,
ht 17.5cm/6¾in, £80–120

▲ Vase by Orrefors
Optical blowing, where a design exploits the refractive and reflective qualities of glass as shown above, is synonymous with the Swedish companies Orrefors and Kosta. The gather of glass was slightly blown, marked with parallel horizontal indentations using glass tweezers, and blown to full size. The smooth outer surface was created by rolling the vase in a damp wood former. Here, the pale blue colour adds to the rippling effect. The base is marked with the factory name and pattern number.

▲ Ice-glass bowl
The crackled effect seen on this unmarked bowl was achieved by dipping the blown bubble of molten glass into cold water. The piece was then completely reheated and expanded, so that the cracks widened and fused back into the molten glass. The iridescence is closely associated with a type of brightly coloured pressed glass, known as "Carnival" glass, made in large quantities in the USA. Such pieces are found in many colours including "gold", "blue", and "green"; the shiny finish is typical of "Carnival" glass. The modest price of this piece makes it an ideal starting point for a novice collector.

Vase by Schneider,
1925, ht 19cm/7in,
£200–300

▼ Vase by Schneider
Another variation on free-blowing was used by the French firm of Schneider to produce this bubbly vase. The gather of clear glass was rolled on the marver into a mixture of crushed glass, grains of colour, and a soda-based substance. The gather was then coated with another layer of clear glass and expanded, so that the soda-based substance produced random air bubbles in the glass. The black foot – a characteristic feature of Schneider glass – was added separately.

Optic moulding

Many designs in the 1920s and 1930s capitalized on the intrinsic reflective and refractive qualities of glass, in particular the way in which it could be blown into a ribbed mould and then expanded to emulate the rippling effect of waves. Most British makers – including Whitefriars Glassworks, Thomas Webb & Sons, and John Walsh Walsh – produced ranges that exploited this quality, and further heightened it by the use of watery colours, especially soft blues, greens, and ambers. Often part of popular, mass-produced ranges, many such pieces were unsigned; however, they can be identified by the colours and wave patterns associated with individual factories.

Vase by Whitefriars, 1920s and 1930s, ht 31cm/12in, **£180–220**

▶ Vase by Whitefriars Glassworks

The wave-like effect on this vase was created by free-blowing the glass into a horizontally ribbed mould, and then into a vertically ribbed mould. Introduced in the 1920s, this design was produced until the end of the 1930s. It was made in three sizes, of which the largest, shown here, is the rarest and most valuable, and in several colours – "sapphire blue" (rarest), "sky blue" (shown here), "yellow", "green", and "red". This pattern was also used on bowls and lamp-bases and was part of a commercially very successful range that is still easily found.

Vase by Webb, 1930s, ht 25cm/9¾in, **£80–120**

▼ Vase by Thomas Webb & Sons

Wave patterns were popular with all the major glass manufacturers. The piece shown here was initially mould-blown to create the continous wave pattern, with the pattern on the glass becoming increasingly elongated towards the bottom of the piece. Webb's colours were more acidic than the softer, more watery ones used by Whitefriars. Amethyst-coloured pieces are in general the rarest and most highly priced, as they fit into what is now a niche collecting area. This example is marked "Thomas Webb".

▼ Decanter by Thomas Webb & Sons

Decanters were usually accompanied by matching glasses. Complete sets are rarely found today, and decanters are highly collectable on their own. The design shown below was mould-blown and then hand-blown; hand-blowing enlarged the piece and expanded the pattern. The coloured stopper was mould-blown to size, so the pattern on it remains crisp, and the mould lines, which can no longer be seen on the decanter, are still clear. The coloured foot was applied separately. "Amethyst" decanters are more popular than green- or yellow-coloured ones.

▼ Vase by Whitefriars Glassworks

The shape of this vase, and its diamond-moulded pattern, were inspired by shards found at a dig at Woodchester Glasshouse, in Gloucestershire, which had been operating in the late 16th and early 17thC. Diamond moulding had also been used by early Venetian glassmakers, and in the 1930s many British companies, including Whitefriars Glassworks, reintroduced the technique. These vases were made in various colours including "sapphire", "gold amber", "green", "sky blue" (shown here), and, most sought after, "sanctuary blue".

Vase by Whitefriars, 1930s, ht 15cm/6in, **£80–120**

▼ Decanter by John Walsh Walsh

Wrythen ribbing was another old Venetian technique revived by Whitefriars Glassworks at the end of the 19thC and popular in the 1920s and 1930s. This decanter has been dipped into a mould and then hand-finished to produce squared-off, dimpled sides. It is part of the "Old Venetian Suite" in the Walsh catalogue of 1929, but these ribbed, dimpled tablewares were so popular that they were made by most major manufacturers. Most are unmarked and relatively affordable.

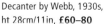
Decanter by Webb, 1930s, ht 28cm/11in, **£60–80**

Decanter by Walsh, 1929, ht 27.5cm/ 10¾in, **£100–120**

Studio glass

Before 1920 there was a clear distinction between glass designer and glassmaker. One of the first to combine the two roles was Maurice Marinot, a French painter and sculptor who began experimenting with glass in 1911 and in 1913 exhibited glass he had designed and produced himself. A fellow Frenchman, Henri Navarre, inspired by Marinot's work, began to produce studio glass in 1924, and was joined by André Thuret, who went on to work alone at the Alfortville Glassworks near Paris. The one-off luxury pieces produced by these artist-craftsmen are rare, very sought after, and correspondingly highly priced; they represent the pinnacle of blown-glass design, and prices reflect their exclusivity and their technical difficulty.

Perfume bottle
by Marinot,
1924, ht
12.5cm/5in,
£3,000–5,000

◀ **Perfume bottle
by Marinot**
The thick glass and internal bubbly decoration of this blown perfume bottle may well have inspired the cased bubbly glass widely produced by British manufacturers (see pp.16–19). This bottle is a classic example of Marinot's range of small, simple forms with tiny clear-glass stoppers, and also features his characteristic profusion of air bubbles. It is marked with Marinot's etched signature, together with a paper label numbered "849", referring to the inventory drawn up by his daughter Florence (the only archive material to have survived the bombing of Marinot's workshop in World War II).

◀ **Perfume bottle
by Marinot**
The time and effort expended by Marinot on his glass explains its rarity and high value. This red perfume bottle (inventory number 1808) took over a year to make, being blown, cased in clear glass, and, over time, repeatedly dipped in hydrofluoric acid to produce the highly controlled, deeply etched decoration. Such exclusive one-off pieces were status symbols in their day, and they remain extremely rare and correspondingly valuable.

Perfume bottle
by Marinot,
mid-1920s,
ht 11.5cm/
4½in,
£15,000–20,000

Vase by Navarre, c.1927,
ht 12.5cm/4¾in, **£800–1,200**

▲ Vase by Navarre

Navarre, who trained as an
architect and a sculptor, began
to experiment with glass in
1924 and from c.1930 was
making simple pieces with
thick, heavy walls and coloured
internal decoration. His designs
are almost as rare and valuable
as those by Marinot (by whom
he was inspired).

▼ Bowl by Marinot

Although classed as a
bowl, the design shown below
is primarily a piece of
sculpture. It is one of the few
larger pieces produced by
Marinot, probably because
such a heavy item would have
been extremely difficult to
support during production.
Marinot has combined great
technical and imaginative skill
to create a sophisticated piece
of artistic, colourless, bubbly
glass, and this is reflected in
its high value. The piece is
signed and has the inventory
number 1808.

Bowl by Marinot, 1929, ht
10.5cm/4in, **£4,000–6,000**

▼ Perfume bottle by Thuret

Thuret's work is either free-
blown (as in this case) or
mould-blown. The technique
of sandwiching a layer of
coloured glass between two
layers of clear glass demanded
great technical expertise; if
misjudged the coloured layers
would splinter, rather like a
car windscreen. Most pieces
are signed "André Thuret".

Perfume bottle by Thuret,
c.1930, ht 21.5cm/8½in,
£2,000–3,000

Major European cased glass

Cased glass is composed of two or more blown layers of differently coloured glass, one of which is often clear. The technique can be combined with trailing, cutting, engraving, acid-etching, and trapped air bubbles to produce highly decorative designs. In the 1920s and 1930s the Loetz glassworks in Vienna produced a range of extremely collectable and very influential cased glass in bold Art Deco forms and bright, contrasting colours. In Sweden master craftsmen at the Orrefors and Kosta glassworks developed the "Graal" and "Ariel" ranges that are now recognized as the early masterpieces of cased glass; such wares are very highly priced, compared with pieces of the same design manufactured after World War II.

Vase by Loetz, early 1920s, ht 30cm/9¾in, **£800–1,200**

▶ **Vase by Loetz**
The bold, simple form, strong contrasting colours, and high-quality glass seen on this vase are hallmarks of a range of simple cased glass made by Loetz in the 1920s. An orange gather of glass was rolled on the marver to collect the black canes that form the decoration, and the gather was then cased in clear glass and blown to size and shape. In general, larger and more complex forms are more highly priced than smaller, simpler pieces. Although unsigned, Loetz designs can be identified from factory records.

Loetz-style vase, 1930s, ht 21cm/8in, **£50–150**

▼ **Loetz-style vase**
With its bold design and strong contrasting colours this simple cased vase from Czechoslovakia (now the Czech Republic) could well be mistaken for a piece by Loetz. The technique used to produce it was very similar to that used to produce the genuine Loetz piece shown left, although the decoration was made by drawing the black glass up the vase rather than rolling it. The clue to the origins of this piece lies in the finishing – the flat-cut top lacks the smooth rounded edge of the real Loetz piece. Nevertheless this remains a good example, very much in the style of the period, and without doubt more affordable than a vase by Loetz.

"Graal" bowl,
1975, diam.
18cm/7in,
£300–400

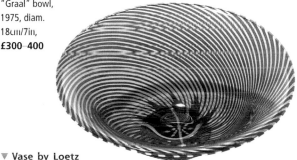

▼ Vase by Loetz

This stylish vase has been
made extra glamorous by the
addition of iridescence and a
crackled effect to the first layer
of pink glass (also cased in
clear glass). The charming
black bun feet would have
been added at a later stage.
This piece may well have been
designed by one of the
distinguished designers of the
Wiener Werkstätte ("Vienna
Workshops") such as Josef
Hoffman, Otto Prutscher,
or Michael Powolny, all of
whom designed glass for the
company, although their
pieces are unsigned.

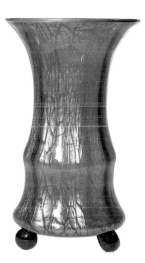

Vase by Loetz,
c.1920, ht
22.5cm/8¾in,
£1,000–1,400

▲ "Graal" bowl

"Graal" glass was developed
for Orrefors in 1916 by the
designer Simon Gate with
the master glassblower Knut
Bergkvist. The complex
technique involves casing a
gather of clear glass in a layer
of glass of another colour,
expanding it to a bubble,
cooling it until cold,
engraving or cutting away
the top colour to form the
decoration, reheating the
glass, casing it in clear glass,
and then expanding it to the
desired shape. Such pieces
demanded supreme
craftsmanship and were
very costly to
make. This bowl
is signed "Orrefors
S. Graal nr.1924
E.5. Edvard Hald"
– "Hald" is the
name of the
designer.

- "Graal" and "Ariel"
are exclusive to Orrefors
and Kosta and are
masterpieces of
glassmaking; later pieces,
made after World War
II, are more modestly
priced than genuine Art
Deco examples.
- Good condition is
essential. Pieces should
have a smooth,
unblemished, shiny finish
– any deviation in line
or rough areas suggest
a chip may have been
polished out. Check for
shear cracks within the
glass by holding the
piece up to the light.

▼ "Ariel" bowl

The technique for producing
"Ariel" glass, developed c.1930
by Bergkvist, Edvin Öhrström,
and Vicke Lindstrand, was
similar to that used to make
"Graal", but was employed on
much thicker glass and with
one or more colour casings.
Early "Graal" and "Ariel" pieces
are prohibitively highly priced
for the novice collector. Post-
war pieces inspired by 1930s
design, as
shown here,
use exactly
the same
technique
but are
far more
modestly
priced.

"Ariel" bowl,
c.1950, ht 18cm/
7in, **£600–800**

Monart cased glass

In 1924 the Moncrieff Glassworks in Perth, Scotland – until then primarily manufacturers of scientific glass – launched a new range of art glass, known as "Monart". The range was the brainchild of Mrs Moncrieff, who collaborated with the highly talented Spanish glassblower Salvador Ysart to produce a variety of clear-cased, internally decorated wares in many different colours and patterns. Some pieces reflect Mrs Moncrieff's passion for Chinese design, particularly in their oriental-inspired forms. Although scientific glass remained the firm's major output, with Monart never exceeding ten per cent of the total production, the range was manufactured from 1924 until 1961 with a break during World War II; it is avidly sought after by collectors today.

▼ **"Pull-up" vase**
Monart pieces were all produced using the same basic technique. A gather of clear glass was rolled on a marver covered with small shards of coloured glass and then cased in clear glass, so that the colour was sandwiched between two layers of clear glass.

The pattern shown here was created using a tool to "pull up" the layer of coloured glass; this produced what became a classic Monart design that was used on a wide range of different shapes. Monart wares were never signed, but were marked instead with a paper label on the base.

"Pull-up" vase, 1930s, ht 27.5cm/10¾in, **£240–280**

▶ **"Nebulae" vase**
The foot of this vase shows the dark, marvered effect produced before the molten glass was expanded by blowing to create the soft, cloudy "Nebulae" pattern. Although this colour scheme was very popular, the lop-sided rim on this piece detracts from its value – had the shape been symmetrical, this vase would be worth between £320 and £380. Although all Monart colours and shapes have been recorded in company catalogues, the random element involved in free-blowing a coloured piece means that no two such items are ever identical.

"Nebulae" vase, 1930s, ht 18cm/7in, **£200–250**

▼ Aventurine bowl

Large shards of glass, known as "pebbles" or "slabs", were used to create the coloured pattern featured on this thick-walled glass bowl. Strong colour and bold form make this piece very attractive to collectors, as do the aventurine inclusions (sparkling metallic particles), which add gold flecks to the pattern and accentuate the marble or stone effect of the thick glass and classical form.

▼ Blown bowl

The pattern on this bowl, which combines colour and air bubbles, is one of the rarer Monart designs and therefore highly sought after. The powdered glass was set out in lines on the marver, and the gather of clear glass was rolled onto the powder before being dipped into a mould to produce the ribbed effect, and then cased. "Red" is the most sought-after colour but is comparatively rare as it is a difficult colour to produce.

Blown bowl, 1930s, ht 10cm/4in, **£400–500**

▼ "Paisley shawl" vase

"Paisley shawl" is another rare pattern used on Monart glass. Here, the vase has been re-marvered to create an extra layer of colour and mica (a mineral giving a shiny finish), and then tooled to produce the swirling, slightly iridescent pattern. This combination of internal cased and external decoration is rare and valuable, and such colourful pieces are keenly collected. Two other highly collectable patterns that use the same technique are "Cloisonné" and "Stoneware".

Aventurine bowl, 1930s, diam. 25.5cm/10in, **£220–280**

"Paisley shawl" vase, 1930s, ht 24cm/10in, **£1,400–1,800**

Other British cased glass

The success of the beautiful coloured-and-cased glass produced by the Moncrieff Glassworks inspired many similar ranges from a large number of other British factories. All of these companies used slightly different patterns and colours, and this helps collectors to identify unmarked pieces. Such major manufacturers as the Whitefriars Glassworks produced notable designs, including the "Cloudy" range; small family firms such as Nazeing also produced attractive pieces, and these wares are still very modestly priced, because so little is known about them. However, the company that was closest in spirit and style to Monart was the London firm of Gray-Stan, a small art-glass workshop that produced a range of well-documented, sought-after, handmade, coloured-and-cased glass.

▶ **"Cloudy" vase by Whitefriars Glassworks**
Between 1928 and 1939, Whitefriars Glassworks produced a series of bowls and vases in coloured glass with small air bubbles that produced a distinctive "cloudy" pattern. The bucket-shaped piece shown here is the most affordable form in the range; oriental-inspired forms are worth at least half or twice as much again. Colours included the brilliant "sanctuary blue" shown here, "green", "yellow", and "red" (rarest). Two-colour combinations are very sought after. Although unmarked, the shapes, colours, and patterns are all identifiable from the firm's catalogues and archives.

"Cloudy" vase, 1930s, ht 20cm/8in, £180–220

Vase by Gray-Stan, 1930s, ht 25cm/9¾in, £180–220

▼ **Vase by Gray-Stan**
In 1926 Mrs Graydon-Stannus launched Gray-Stan art glass from her Battersea factory. Although many forms, including the classic, elegant, Chinese-style vase shown here, are reminiscent of Monart, Gray-Stan pieces have a much more powdery finish and use a different colour palette. Gray-Stan wares, made until 1936, must be signed for premium value, although the large number of unsigned pieces can be identified from existing signed pieces.

Vase by Gray-Stan, 1930s, ht 25cm/9¾in, **£400–450**

▲ Vase by Gray-Stan

The characteristic swirling, powdery Gray-Stan pattern is seen here in "red" – a rare and sought-after colour that was unstable when heated and inherently difficult to produce. The dimpled sides are reminiscent of successful designs by Whitefriars Glassworks and John Walsh Walsh, and were very popular in the 1930s. A combination of large size, rare colour, and the Gray-Stan signature in script explain the high value of this piece.

Vase by Nazeing, 1930s, ht 23cm/9in, **£100–140**

▲ Vase by Nazeing

Little is known about the Nazeing glass produced in the 1930s, as there are no company archives for that period. Extensive handling of items known to have been supplied to retailers by Nazeing is therefore the most reliable form of attribution. This piece features the characteristic "cloudy" pattern dotted with tiny bubbles that is a reliable identifying feature of glass by this firm.

▼ Vase by Nazeing

Although this amethyst-coloured vase is similar to some Monart shapes, the over-large foot and wide, flaring rim combined with the distinctive "cloudy" pattern identify it as Nazeing glass. This is a very attractive piece and a good starting-point for a novice collector as it is relatively affordable. Many Nazeing pieces are modestly priced at present because comparatively little is known about the firm's Art Deco production. With all pieces, check carefully for chips or blemishes to what should be a smooth uniform surface.

Vase by Nazeing, 1930s, ht 18cm/7in, **£80–120**

Other cased glass

Bubbly, marvered cased glass was also very popular in Europe, and the wide range of wares produced offers great scope to collectors. Among the leading exponents in France was Schneider, whose vases and bowls were celebrated at the 1925 Paris Exposition Internationale des Arts Décoratifs et Industriels Modernes ("International Exhibition of Decorative and Modern Industrial Arts"). Glassworks in Czechoslovakia (now the Czech Republic) also made cased glass, although their pieces tend to fall into two distinct categories: a high-quality range comparable to good French and British pieces, and less-inspired, very commercial glass. In Germany the Württemberg Metalwork Factory ("WMF"), although better known for Art Nouveau metalwork, produced some art glass, notably pieces by such top freelance designers as Wilhelm Wagenfeld. In The Netherlands the Leerdam factory also owed much of its success to talented designers, among them Andries Dirk Copier.

▼ **"Jades" vase by Schneider**
The elegant, elongated form of this pebble-marvered, blown "Jades" vase is typical of Schneider, as are the stoneware effect and applied dark-red handles. However, the satin-matt finish is rare and was probably created by sandblasting the glass and then polishing it with a weak acid. This design was produced in quantity and is readily available, unlike the vase shown right. The piece on the left is signed "Schneider" in script; the company name is sometimes found in block capitals, and some pieces are also marked "Le Verre Français".

"Jades" vase, 1920s,
ht 30cm/11¾in, **£400–500**

▶ **Vase by Schneider**
A more refined version of the vase shown left can be seen in the rare piece shown right. Here the applied handles have been extended into elegant tears, and the typical black foot has become part of an archetypally bold Art Deco colour combination – red with a white cased body decorated with internal bubbles. The engraved company mark is clearly visible.

Vase by Schneider, 1925, ht 18cm/7in, **£2,000–3,000**

Bowl by WMF,
c.1933, diam.
25.5cm/
10in, **£70–90**

▼ Lamp-base
This mould-blown, cased,
bubbly glass lamp-base was
manufactured by an unknown
factory in Czechoslovakia, and
would originally have been
worth little more than £40
to £60. A number of very
similar pieces have been
found complete with paper
labels identifying the factory,
which may well have supplied
many different retail outlets.
With the presence of such
labels and
attribution
possible, the
value of the
piece has
trebled.

▲ Bowl by WMF
This blown bowl combines
several decorative techniques.
Strips of coloured glass were
rolled on a marver onto a
clear gather of glass, which
was then ribbed in a mould
before being plunged into
cold water to create the
crackled effect. The piece
would then have been
reheated and expanded to
enhance the ribbed design and
bring out the flame like strips
of colour and the crackled
effect. This combination of
effects is thought to be
exclusive to WMF, whose
pieces are often unsigned.

▼ "Serica" vase by Leerdam
In 1923 Copier joined
Leerdam as principal designer,
and was responsible for two of
their studio ranges: "Unica",
which consisted of one-off
pieces only, and "Serica", a
series of limited-edition vases,
with characteristic thick walls
and internal decoration of
bubbles or "seaweed" patterns.
Leerdam Art Deco pieces are
rare and are as highly
priced today as they were
in the 1920s. Most
pieces in the "Unica"
and "Serica" ranges
are marked with the
name of the factory,
the designer, and the
series. This example
is marked "SERICA
COPIER".

Lamp-base, 1930s,
ht 20cm/8in, **£150–180**

"Serica" vase by Leerdam,
1927, ht 20cm/8in, **£300–400**

Iridescent glass

Inspired by excavations of Roman glass with an iridescent finish caused by a reaction with metal oxides during burial, in 1878 the British firm of Thomas Webb & Sons patented a process for iridizing contemporary glass by exposing it to fumes of metal oxides. The technique, which subsequently involved painting or spraying glass with lustrous colours that became shiny when heated, was developed and refined in Vienna by Loetz and in the USA by Louis Comfort Tiffany. Loetz and Tiffany glass are keenly collected and valuable; iridescent glass by other manufacturers is more modestly priced and readily found. In the 1920s and 1930s iridescent glass was closely associated with Art Nouveau; it tended to wane in popularity with the emergence of bubbly cased glass.

▶ **"Amethyst" vase**
Although unmarked, this "amethyst" vase with silvered spots and a crimped top was almost certainly made in Bohemia (now part of the Czech Republic), as the form is typical of many wares in 19thC British styles made in Bohemia and imported into Britain after World War I. This example was hand-blown and then put into a fume chamber before being finished, and the iridescence is only found on the outside. This vase is a good example of fine quality glass that will be very modestly priced because it is as yet unattributable.

"Amethyst" vase, 1920s, ht 13cm/5in, **£80–120**

▼ **"Fan" vase by John Walsh Walsh**
All-over iridescence, as seen on this blown-and-thrown opalescent vase, is achieved by iridizing after finishing. This shape is very fragile – few examples have survived, and those that have must be in tip-top condition for maximum value. This design was made in several colours: "green" is rarest, "flint" the most commonly found and affordable, and "straw opal", which shows off the typical Walsh mother-of-pearl iridescence to best effect, the most desirable and highly priced. All pieces by this British firm are much more affordable than equivalent pieces made in continental Europe.

"Fan" vase by Walsh, 1900, ht 24cm/9 ½in, **£300–400**

▼ **Vase by Loetz**
Loetz is closely
associated with
iridescent designs with
a characteristic oil-on-
water effect, as shown
on the free-blown piece
below; the blue of this
example is also typical.
However, the combination of
iridescent and plain glass — a
technically difficult two-tone
effect, which is correspondingly
highly priced — is fairly
unusual. Dating can be
problematic, as production of
iridescent glass by Loetz
began before World War I and
continued into the 1920s.

Vase by Loetz, c.1921,
ht 19.5cm/7¾in, **£400–600**

"Cypriote" vase by Tiffany, c.1920,
ht 18cm/7in, **£2,000–3,000**

▲ **"Cypriote" vase by
Tiffany Studios**
The name of Tiffany is
virtually synonymous with
highly stylized, beautifully
finished iridescent Art
Nouveau glass. However,
the company also produced
a range known as "Cypriote"
in free-blown, organic
shapes with a pitted
iridescent surface
that resembled the
decayed and
corroded finish
found on ancient
glass. All Tiffany
pieces are signed,
and this vase bears
the company name
on the base, together
with the letter "P",
indicating a date
of c.1921.

"Gladioli" vase by Tiffany,
c.1920, ht 26.5cm/10½in,
£5,000–7,000

• Iridescent glass is
now produced in large
quantities by studio
glassmakers worldwide,
and it has been
known for work by
contemporary American
and British artists to
be sold as early
iridescent glass.
• The best safeguard is
to buy from a reputable
dealer and ask for a
detailed receipt.
• Pieces by Loetz have
been widely copied,
so collectors should be
particularly cautious of
all designs with Loetz-
style iridescence.

▼ **"Gladioli" vase by
Tiffany Studios**
This vase has been decorated
using two iridizing techniques.
Metal oxides were painted onto
the hot glass to create the floral
decoration, and the piece
was then exposed to a
single vapour to give
an overall iridescence.
Tiffany pieces such
as the example
shown proved very
inspirational to the
American firm of
Quezal, and although
glass by Quezal is
usually signed with
the company name, it
is occasionally found
with a spurious Tiffany
signature. Novice
collectors should seek
professional advice if
in any doubt over
the authenticity.

Applied decoration

Early (15thC) Venetian glassmakers were supreme exponents of applied decoration – the addition of trailed molten glass to a hot glass form, so that when the piece cools, the applied decoration stands proud. Such decoration, although extremely vulnerable, was newly popular in the 19thC, and in the 1920s and 1930s many designs in historical and traditional styles were produced alongside a variety of wares in bold modern styles. Italian glassmakers perpetuated the historical tradition, and in perfect condition their pieces can be very valuable. British factories such as the Whitefriars Glassworks produced both traditional and modern ranges; their pieces in bold Art Deco shapes with trailed decoration are generally more affordable than the glass in historical styles.

▼ Ribbon-trailed vase by Whitefriars Glassworks

Ribbon-trailed vase by Whitefriars, 1935, ht 18cm/7in, **£180–220** (single colour **£50–70**)

Barnaby Powell designed this hand-blown, ribbon-trailed vase for Whitefriars Glassworks in 1935. Its pattern number was 9030, and the two-colour version was produced until 1949. The most commonly found two colour-version is "blue" over "sea green", but "amethyst" over "blue" is also known; two-colour versions are rarer and more desirable than the more commonly found one-colour versions, which were produced until 1964. Each vase is unique because the trailed decoration, which was applied at the top of the vase and then pulled down, differs slightly from piece to piece.

▶ "Strap" vase

This "sky blue" vase with "amethyst" applied decoration was also designed by Powell. The decoration was formed by applying a separately blown bubble to the free-blown body and then pulling the bubble down to flatten it. The clear "eye" at the centre of the tear shows where the bubble was blown onto the glass. This piece is rare, and the colour scheme shown is the only one known. A similar technique was used by the designer Geoffrey Baxter from 1969 until 1971, but in different colours and forms; check the Whitefriars catalogue to avoid confusion.

"Strap" vase, 1934, ht 18cm/7in, **£350–450**

• Good condition is essential, as it is virtually impossible to restore broken or missing decoration successfully.
• Pieces in historical styles generally have elaborate decoration; however, they are very vulnerable and rarely found in top condition.
• Bold, strong forms with applied decoration in contemporary styles are usually more modestly priced and readily found.

Venetian vase, late 1920s, ht 22cm/8¾in, **£30–40**

▲ Venetian vase

The traditional Venetian shape of this free-blown vase is offset by several features that give the piece a distinctly Art Deco feel; most notable are the stylish combination of pinkish glass with black decoration, the eye-catching design and bold application of the nipped swag decoration, and the subtle use of iridescence, probably by spraying. In perfect condition, such a rare piece would command between £300 and £400. However, as a piece of trailing is missing from this example, and this cannot be fully restored (hot glass cannot be applied to cold), the value of the vase is very dramatically reduced.

▼ Threaded bowl

Although designed in the 1920s, the threaded blue decoration on this flint bowl is essentially Victorian rather than Art Deco. The blue glass was thinly trailed onto the hand-blown flint body, starting at the rim where the trail is thicker and darker. The body was then dipped into a ribbed mould, and the thick bun foot, which also has trailing to the underside, was flattened on a wooden board. Other colour schemes known include "red" on "red" (rarest and most valuable), "yellow" on "yellow", and "green" on "green". Designed by William Butler for Whitefriars Glassworks, this vase was produced in five sizes, the smallest of which is shown here.

Threaded bowl, 1920s, ht 10cm/4in, **£80–120**

Römer by Whitefriars, 1931, ht 14.5cm/ 5¾in, **£400–600**

▶ Römer by Whitefriars Glassworks

This *Römer*, inspired by 17thC German drinking glasses with ovoid bowls, cylindrical stems, and flared feet, was designed by Harry Powell. Although made of crystal, this piece has been given a sea-green tinge in the style of the green *Waldglas* ("wood glass"), from which early *Römer* were made. The prunts on the stem were applied as blobs and then shaped with special tools. Very few of these glasses have survived, probably because they were costly to make and not commercially viable.

Pressed & mould-blown glass

Pressed glass is produced by pouring molten glass into a mould and then pushing it down with a plunger to create a moulded exterior and a smooth, hollow interior. The technique was first developed in the 1830s in the USA as a way of mass-producing inexpensive copies of cut glass; it was revived in the 1930s and used to make colourful and now collectable Art Deco vases, figures, and trinket sets by such British companies as Jobling & Co., Bagley Crystal Co., and George Davidson & Co. With mould-blowing – a long-established technique used in the inter-war years to produce a wide range of glass from inexpensive tableware to more exclusive decorative pieces – the gather is blown into a full-size mould (usually two-piece) with deep relief decoration that can be felt on the interior of the piece.

Pressed-glass vase by Jobling, 1930s, ht 25.5cm/ 10in, **£50–70**

◄ **Pressed-glass vase by Jobling & Co.**
This vase, decorated with stylized flowers in relief, is a good example of affordable, underrated, classic Art Deco glass. Such pieces, mostly unmarked, can be researched in trade catalogues and pattern books, although attribution is not essential for full value. This vase would have been designed by an in-house designer and produced in large quantities, which makes it readily available today. Such modestly priced pieces must be in perfect condition to merit attention; always check the insides of vases for limescale build-up, as this is difficult to remove.

▼ **"Koala bear" vase by Bagley Crystal Co.**
Bagley began producing pressed glass in 1912, and by the 1920s was the leading manufacturer of inexpensive domestic pressed glass. Its reputation received a boost in 1934, when it was given the royal seal of approval from Queen Mary. This "Koala bear" vase was probably made for an exhibition or as a limited production run, and is a good example of the complex type of design that could be achieved by pressing.

"Koala bear" vase by Bagley, 1930s, ht 20.5cm/8in, **£400–600**

▼ **Centrepiece vase by Jobling & Co.**

This frosted, pressed-glass centrepiece, one of a range of art-glass designs inspired by Lalique and launched by the firm of Jobling & Co. in 1933, was produced in a variety of pale colours, including "grey/blue", "pink", and, "green". The three pieces that make up such a centrepiece – a bowl, rose, and figure – are rarely found in top condition, and the figure is often missing.

Centrepiece vase by Jobling, late 1930s, ht 30cm/12in, £120–180 (£20–30 without figure)

"Cloud" vase by Davidson, c.1923, ht 25.5cm/10in, **£120–150**

▲ **"Cloud" vase by George Davidson & Co.**

This vase is unmarked, but the mould-blown "Cloud" design, launched in 1922, identifies it as a piece by George Davidson & Co. The swirling effect was produced by stirring the colour before the glass was blown into the mould. Dating is based on colour: "amber" was produced in 1922, "purple" (seen here) in 1923, "tortoiseshell" (least popular) in 1928, "green" in 1933, and "scarlet" and "orange" (rarest) in 1930 and 1934 respectively.

- Look for earlier pieces, as they are more sought after than later ones. Also look for items with crisp design – definition from the mould softens with use.
- Good condition is essential for modestly priced pieces, so avoid vases with limescale build-up.
- Pieces with a frosted finish must be in perfect condition, as chips cannot be removed without losing the frosting.
- Pressed glass is generally unmarked, but attribution is not always essential for maximum value.

▼ **"Lion" vase designed by D'Avesn**

The two sets of vertical lines still present on the upper part of this magnificent, high-quality vase show that it was blown into a two piece mould. Designed by Paul D'Avesn, whose work was strongly influenced by Lalique, it features typically Art Deco stylized "lions". Such a piece easily matches the quality of glass by major French names but is much more affordable. All of D'Avesn' work is signed on the base.

"Lion" vase, c.1930, ht 21cm/8in, **£700–900**

27

Opalescent glass

Thicker areas of glass cool more slowly and retain greater opacity and colour than the thinner areas, which cool more quickly and remain more transparent. Venetian glassmakers exploited this property as early as the 16thC, but in the 1920s and 1930s it was celebrated French makers such as René Lalique and Marius-Ernest Sabino who were leaders in the luxury art-glass market, and whose opalescent pieces are most highly sought after by collectors today. Many other glass manufacturers produced less ambitious ranges of opalescent glass, among them the British company Jobling & Co., and their opalescent wares will be far more readily found and modestly priced.

◄ **Vase by Lalique**

The name Lalique is synonymous with luxury glass, although most pieces were made by the Lalique factory rather than by the man himself. To make this vase, glass was thinly blown into an intricate bronze mould and then enamelled to enhance the opalescent effect. The blue enamel shown was a particularly popular colour. Fired at low temperatures, the enamel is vulnerable and needs to be checked carefully for condition; it may even be missing. Although the bronze mould could be reused many times, such pieces were very valuable then, as now, and are correspondingly rare.

Vase by Lalique, 1920s, ht 16cm/6in, **£800–1,200**

▼ **"Coquilles" bowl and stand by Lalique**

The geometric shell design on this finger bowl and stand is quintessentially Art Deco. Plates and bowls were also produced, and all were press-moulded to provide a smooth eating surface, with the pattern on the underneath of the piece. The plate perfectly shows how opalescent glass is cloudiest in the thicker areas – here in the thicker areas of the shells. A complete set of six finger bowls and stands would be worth at least double the value of the two pieces shown. Note the wheel-engraved signature "R. Lalique" in the centre.

"Coquilles" bowl and stand by Lalique, c.1930, diam. of stand 17cm/6¾in, **£80–100**

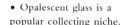

▼ Butterfly by Sabino

Small figures and animals are now among the most popular of Sabino's range of opalescent pressed-glass wares that also included bowls, vases, trinket boxes, menu-holders, and ashtrays. The two-piece moulds meant that the decoration appeared on both sides of the piece (unlike on the "Coquilles" service shown left). Many of these moulds, carrying the mark "Sabino Made in France", are still in existence, and are used today to produce small birds and animals. The only way to make sure that the piece was made in the 1920s and 1930s is to check the Sabino catalogue carefully to see which moulds were destroyed during the war.

Butterfly by Sabino, 1930s,
ht 15cm/6in, **£200–300**

▼ Bowl by Jobling & Co.

In 1933 Jobling & Co. introduced a range of pressed glass inspired by Lalique. The stylized birds on this bowl show a French influence, and the long-standing British tradition of fine mould-making can be seen in the attention to detail. This bowl is a good example of the fine pieces produced by British makers that are undervalued at present, although the situation is changing following recent exhibitions of 1920s and 1930s British glass. The design shown was registered (marked "Reg. no. 780717"), which meant that it could only be used for a limited period.

Bowl by Jobling, c.1934,
diam. 18cm/7in,
£140–180

- Opalescent glass is a popular collecting niche.
- Although Lalique is the best-known and most sought-after maker, many other pieces by lesser-known names are equally good and much more affordable.
- Later Lalique pieces from original moulds may have been "aged" by the addition of an R to the mark.
- Condition is vital – buy nothing with a chip or crack, as opalescent glass cannot be restored to its original finish.

▼ Salt and pepper pots

These opalescent, fish-shaped salt and pepper pots with screw-on noses are typical of the small, humorous pieces produced by many factories in the north-east of England in the 1920s and 1930s. However, such items are now rare as they were often thrown away as soon as they were damaged. Today such novelty designs are very popular because they are inexpensive, easy to display, practical, and, above all, great fun. Few examples are marked.

Salt and pepper pots, 1930s, l. 5cm/2in,
£80–120 (for the pair) or **£30–40** (individually)

Pâte-de-verre

Pâte-de-verre ("glass paste") is a complex and costly technique used to create one-off and limited-edition pieces. A wax dummy of a design is enclosed in plaster, and the wax is steamed off to leave behind a plaster mould; the mould is filled with crushed glass in various colours, which is heated until it fuses, then cooled and removed from the mould. The technique, which was first used in Ancient Egypt, was rediscovered by the French sculptor Henri Cros. His experiments with powdered glass in 1884, and the discovery of the tomb of Tutankhamun in 1923, sparked a fashion for *pâte-de-verre* and Egyptian forms, a field in which French makers excelled. These French craftsmen in turn inspired Frederick Carder, one of the major names in the glassmaking world; Carder's *pâte-de-verre* pieces are even more rare and highly priced than the exclusive, experimental designs of his European counterparts.

▼ Vase by Décorchemont

François-Emile Décorchemont, a ceramicist turned glassmaker, experimented with *pâte-de-verre* as early as 1902, but it was not until after World War I that he became well known for large, thick-walled vases with surface decoration in rich, veined, streaky and bubbled colours. Typically this vase has geometric decoration on the textured exterior, and a smooth interior. From 1912 all Décorchemont wares were marked with a signature and a number.

Vase by Décorchement, 1930, ht 13cm/5in, **£3,000–5,000**

▼ Cup by Argy-Rousseau

The other leading designer of *pâte-de-verre* was Joseph-Gabriel Argy-Rousseau, also a former ceramicist. In 1921 he and a partner established Les Pâtes-de-Verres d'Argy-Rousseau, a small workshop in Paris, where they produced small, richly coloured pieces. Early examples – such as this *coupe aux raisins* ("grape cup") – were decorated with the fruits, flowers, and natural motifs synonymous with Art Nouveau. Later pieces incorporated geometric designs typically associated with Art Deco.

Cup by Argy-Rousseau, 1926, ht 9cm/3in, **£1,500–2,000**

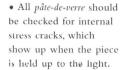

Dish by Walter,
1920s, ht 17cm/
6¾in, **£3,000–
4,000**

▼ Vase by Argy-
Rousseau

This vase is made of a
translucent glass known as
pâte-de-cristal. The plain form
with simple geometric
decoration inspired by archaic
motifs is similar to pieces by
Décorchemont, but can be
clearly identified as Argy-
Rousseau because it is more
translucent, finer, and has
none of the veining associated
with Décorchemont's glass.
This piece also has an impressed
mark and can be found in the
1927 Argy-Rousseau catalogue.

▲ Dish by Walter

The workshop established
by Alméric Walter in 1919 is
now best known for a range
of figural and animal pieces
that were produced both
as individual sculptures
and applied to ashtrays,
paperweights, and vases.
The smaller pieces have a
sensuous smooth, silky finish
and are relatively affordable.
Walter commissioned designs
from a number of artists,
whose signatures often
appear on their pieces,
or on the maquette. The
mark "A. Walter Nancy"
was used from 1919.

Vase by Argy Rousseau,
1927, ht 13cm/5in,
£1,800–2,200

▼ Plaque by Carder

Frederick Carder was chief
designer at Stevens & Williams
before he moved to the USA,
where from 1903 he worked
for the Steuben Glassworks.
He experimented with all
types of glassmaking, but his
pâte-de-verre pieces, such as
this plaque, are
among the rarest
examples of his work.
So few pieces are
available on the
market that it is
almost impossible to
assess their value.

Plaque by Carder,
c.1930s, ht 23cm/9in,
from **£5,000**

British cut glass

Although little change was made to the basic technique of cutting glass with a stone wheel, used since Roman times, by 1920 the firm of Stuart & Sons Ltd had replaced the final hand polish on its cut glass with an acid polish that gave a much brighter, shinier finish. This lustrous look was ideally suited to the bold shapes and deep, intricate, stylized cuttings that were used for abstract geometric Art Deco motifs. Although glassmakers in Bohemia (now part of the Czech Republic) were also highly skilled in making these valuable heavy Art Deco vases, bowls, and decanters, their work is now so rare as to be virtually unobtainable; instead such British firms as Thomas Webb & Sons and Stevens & Williams are at the forefront of the collecting field.

Vase by Stuart, 1935, ht 23.5cm/9¼in, **£80–120**

▼ **Vase by Stuart & Sons Ltd**
Ludwig Kny, the son of a talented Bohemian glass engraver, became chief designer at Stuart & Sons Ltd after World War I. Although, as he was a staff designer, his pieces are not always signed, they are instantly recognizable by the distinctive cutting technique, in which the outside edges of the broad cuts are then further cut with an intaglio wheel to create a brilliant refracting surface. His work, such as this hand-blown "golden amber" vase, although previously somewhat underrated, is now beginning to attract the attention it deserves.

▼ **Bowl by Stuart & Sons Ltd**
The high lead content of Stuart glass gives it a refractive and reflective quality that is ideally suited to the spectacular classic Art Deco sunburst motif featured on this rare bowl, which was also designed by Kny. Such deep and broad mitre cutting would have demanded at least 4cm (1½in) of solid glass at the bottom, which would in turn have demanded an extremely strong glassblower. The company mark appears on the bottom of this piece.

Bowl by Stuart, 1935, diam. 28.5cm/11in, **£200–300**

▼ Vase by Stuart & Sons Ltd

Company records reveal that this unmarked, mould-blown vase was designed by A.R. Pearce. However, the combination of a strong form, bold design, and skilful cutting is more important than attribution. The cuts for the waves were made first and acid-polished before the stylized, three-cut, matt birds were added. The contrast between thick and thin lines in the wave-shaped cuts add to the feeling of movement, and the contrast in texture between shiny and matt glass creates a sense of depth and perspective.

Vase by Stuart, 1939, ht 20cm/8in,
£150–200

▼ Cocktail shaker by Stuart & Sons Ltd

Cocktail shakers and glasses are lasting and highly popular symbols of the hedonism of the inter-war years. Complete sets of shaker and six glasses are rare and highly priced (£700–800), but individual pieces are collectable in their own right, and single glasses are often affordable (£30–50 each). This mould-blown shaker with a fish-and-waves motif was one of the Stuart pieces made for the British Art in Industry Exhibition in 1935. It is cut in the style designed by Kny, whose mark ("L.Kny") appears on the base, together with the company name.

▼ Vase by Thomas Webb & Sons

This cased vase was designed by Anna Fogelberg and made by Webb for the Rembrandt Guild. Although black and clear glass was a popular Art Deco combination, black glass is rare, and most so-called "black" glass is in fact a very dark "amethyst", as true black is inherently unstable and difficult to produce.

Vase by Webb, c 1935, ht 24.5cm/9¾in,
£300–400

Cocktail shaker by Stuart,
c.1934, ht 22.5cm/8¾in,
£250–350

Vase by Walsh, c.1935,
ht 25.5cm/10in, **£200–300**

Decanter by
Murray for Royal
Brierley, 1934,
ht 34cm/13¼in,
£700–900

Vase by Whitefriars, c.1935,
ht 31cm/12in, **£400–600**

▲ Vase by Whitefriars Glassworks

Designed in 1935 and made until 1937, this hand-blown vase in "sapphire blue" ("gold amber" was the other colour frequently used) is a classic example of one of Whitefriars' upmarket, one-off pieces. Although designs by this firm are unsigned, detailed archive material and comprehensive exhibition-catalogue records make attribution possible; however, misattribution is becoming increasingly common following the enthusiastic response to the highly successful Whitefriars' exhibition of 1996/7.

▲ Vase by John Walsh Walsh

The Neo-Georgian cut glass by this firm was supplemented by a more innovative selection of Art Deco glass, of which the vase above is a good example. It is decorated with the "Kendal" pattern – vertical, shallow-cut "leaf" shapes, spanned by engraved arched lines – which was also used on decanters and tumblers. This vase, which was made in two sizes, was designed by W. Clyne Farquharson, whose signature, along with the factory name, appears on the base; later examples are marked "Tudor". As a well-documented piece, this is a good starting-point for any collector.

▲ Decanter by Murray for Royal Brierley

This hand-blown decanter was designed by Keith Murray for Stevens & Williams (known as "Royal Brierley" after receiving a royal warrant from George V). It is an example of one of Murray's rare, heavily cut designs. The horizontal step-cutting was an extremely difficult and costly technique, as any flaw in the glass spelled disaster. Any Murray piece is highly sought after and must be attributable on the basis of a signature, or from published designs, or by a written receipt from a reputable dealer.

▼ Basket by Royal Brierley

The chinoiserie "Willow" pattern featured on this blown-and-cased crystal fruit basket was the hallmark of T.E. Wood, a freelance decorator, who used the design on clear and cased glass. This basket combines a typical Art Deco motif (chinoiserie designs were all the rage during the period) with traditional cutting on the handle, and in this case the combination works well. The "Willow" pattern" is usually found in "blue" ("red" is rare), and is especially sought after by American collectors. The price of this piece reflects both the design's popularity and the higher prices paid for cased glass.

Royal Brierley basket, 1930s, ht 20cm/8in, **£600–800**

◀ Vase by Harbridge Crystal Co. Ltd

Harbridge Crystal Co. Ltd was a small glass factory about which little is known. Such small firms were to a large degree eclipsed by major makers, although their wares now have the attraction of being very similar in style to those by big names, but far more modestly priced. The vase shown is an odd combination of two different traditions; the naturalistic, curving leaf-cutting is typical of the 1920s and 1930s, but it is rather incongruously topped by traditional mitre-cutting around the rim, and there is an equally traditional star-cut foot. However, the piece is well-made, signed, and an interesting example of the marriage of two styles popular in the 1930s.

- Collect by good, bold design rather than name. Many good pieces are unattributable, because small factories did not always mark their pieces.
- Well-documented pieces are a safe starting-point, as they are likely to maintain their prices.
- Cased glass is rarer and more highly priced than uncased glass; large cased examples, in particular, may command a premium.
- Bowls are often lightly scratched, but a piece that scratches easily can be just as easily restored – scratches simply need to be carefully polished away.

Vase by Harbridge Crystal, 1935, ht 25.5cm/10in, **£40–60**

Other cut glass

European manufacturers were far more willing to embrace the new Art Deco style than their British counterparts. Swedish designers were among the first to exploit the optical effects created by cutting thick, clear glass, and the striking results have a timeless modernity that transcends collecting niches. Some of the long-established French glassmaking companies, such as Baccarat, produced stylish cut-glass pieces that are quintessentially Deco. In Vienna the Lobmeyr glassworks commissioned designs from artists associated with the Wiener Werkstätte ("Vienna Workshops"), among them Josef Hoffmann. Marked pieces by such companies are eagerly sought after, and collectors who are prepared to buy unattributed pieces may well find superb examples at modest prices.

Vase by
Orrefors,
designed
1932, ht
14.5cm/5¾in,
£200–300

◀ **Vase by Orrefors**

This vase, designed by Simon Gate for the Swedish firm of Orrefors, stylishly combines a black foot with a clear crystal body cut in the "1000 Windows" pattern. The effect, similar to that of a hall of mirrors, is obtained by cutting five deep vertical mitres and a series of undercut semi-circles into clear glass that is almost 1cm (⅜in) thick. The polished base is marked "OFGA 395/3", identifying the company, the designer, and the pattern. All items attributed to Orrefors should be carefully checked against the firm's detailed design records.

▼ **Vase by Orrefors**

Another example of Gate's innovative use of the reflective and refractive properties of glass can be seen in this small mould-blown vase. The rows of polished circles (known as "printies") on the thick (1.3cm/½in) glass act as lenses, creating thousands of polished bubbles, which are offset by small matt spots. The design is less well known than "1000 Windows", shown left, and is often overlooked, which makes it correspondingly modestly priced for such a dramatic design. This example is clearly signed "Orrefors Sweden" and marked "GA 1695".

Vase by
Orrefors,
designed
1937, ht
11.5cm/4½in,
£50–70

Candelabrum by Baccarat, 1930s, ht 15cm/6in, **£1,500–2,000**

▲ Candelabrum by Baccarat

Designed for Baccarat by Jacques Adnet, the cast candelabrum shown above is a wonderful example of French Art Deco at its best. The piece features a silvered bronze base and top, with four geometric cast, then hand finished, cut glass arms – a combination of materials that was popularly used in Art Deco lighting design. Such candlesticks are rare and valuable, and few have survived unscathed, as the candles often burnt down into the unprotected glass arms and caused irreparable cracks. A safer compromise was the use of metal candle holders within the glass arms, although this is usually less aesthetically pleasing than all-glass arms. On this example the company name is etched in the bronze base.

"Ruby" vase, 1930s, ht 15cm/6in, **£120–160**

▲ "Ruby" vase

There are several clues to the origins of this unmarked and unidentified hand-blown, cased vase. The slightly pink tone of the "ruby" glass is reminiscent of designs made by glassworks in France or the Val-Saint-Lambert Glasshouse in Belgium, as opposed to the cranberry tone of "ruby" glass made in Britain or Bohemia (now part of the Czech Republic). The highly stylized design suggests that this piece was produced in the 1930s (glass made in the 1920s still had a strong Art Nouveau influence). This piece is a fine example of good design and skilled cutting, and represents excellent value for money.

Bowl by Hoffmann, 1920s, ht 10.5cm/4¼in, **£400–600**

▲ Bowl by Hoffmann

This bowl was designed by Josef Hoffmann, a leading Austrian architect and designer and one of the founder members of the Wiener Werkstätte, possibly for the Viennese firm of Lobmeyr. The piece was probably mould-blown and then cut. The thick walls and chunky geometric design are characteristic features of Hoffmann's work.

British engraved glass

In the inter-war years, inexpensive glass made in Czechoslovakia (now the Czech Republic) flooded the lower end of the market, so major British firms such as John Walsh Walsh, Thomas Webb & Sons, and Stevens & Williams concentrated on a range of luxury glass that combined cutting and engraving (a much shallower form of cutting, usually with a copper wheel). There were two major styles of decoration: the first looked back to Art Nouveau and used sinuous flower and plant motifs; the second, influenced by Swedish glassmakers and the new Art Deco style, used more graphic, stylized motifs. Both styles are highly sought after, but pieces that combine or confuse the two are less popular among collectors.

▼ Vase by John Walsh Walsh

This art-glass vase was free-blown, allowing the glass blower to control the weight and thickness of the glass to produce the darker foot to represent the water, with the colour gradually becoming lighter as the glass becomes thinner towards the rim. It was made in several sizes and colours, including "yellow" and "blue". The decorative motif of water lilies and irises in a pond has been skilfully executed with horizontal cuts for the water, and a classic combination of polished and matt engraving for the irises, the outlines of which have been intaglio cut, acid-polished, and then matt-engraved.

Vase by Walsh, 1930s, ht 25.5cm/10in, **£250–350**

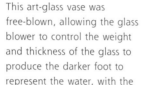

▼ "Gay glass" bowl by Thomas Webb & Sons

The luxury "Gay glass" range was launched in 1933. The "Cut Water Lily" pattern shown here was the most sought after of the four different designs in the range, and was used on vases and bowls. The pattern came in four different colour schemes: "Spring" (eau-de-nil green), "Evergreen" (dark green), "Sunshine" (a distinctive golden-amber shade made using uranium, and probably the most popular colour), and "Crystal" (seen here). This mould-blown example has the acid-etched company mark on the side.

"Gay glass" bowl by Webb, 1933–9, ht 10cm/4in, **£140–160**

"Cactus" vase by Webb, 1935, ht 20cm/8in, **£1,200–1,800**

▲ **"Cactus" vase by Thomas Webb & Sons**
Designed by Anna Fogelberg, this blown clear-glass vase with a stylish black foot offers a complete contrast to the Art Nouveau-influenced bowl shown left. The deeply engraved "cacti" around the base may have been inspired by the vogue for Hollywood Westerns. This design was produced exclusively for the Rembrandt Guild and is very rare; it may even have been a prototype that never went into production because it was too costly to produce or too modern for the more traditional British taste. This piece is marked "Webb Made in England" and "Made Exclusively for Rembrant Guild".

▼ **"Cactus" vase by Murray for Stevens & Williams**
This vase, designed by Keith Murray, would have been hard to produce because of its large size and weight – holding a vase made of such thick glass during the engraving process would have been very arduous. Murray produced a series of cactus designs for this firm, mostly for vases, although two decanters are also known. All examples are very rare; some are unmarked and unsigned. However, the lack of a mark is not problematic, as all Murray designs can be identified from archive material.

"Cactus" vase by Murray for Stevens & Williams, c.1935, ht 38cm/15in, **£2,000–3,000**

▼ **Cocktail shaker by Stuart & Sons Ltd**
Designed by Dame Laura Knight, this Scandinavian-influenced cocktail shaker was one of the pieces shown at an exhibition held at the London department store of Harrods in 1934. All the glass was made by Stuart, which was commissioned by the government to produce tableware designed by top artists in an attempt to promote good glass design. All items shown were marked with the name of the firm and the designer, and are very desirable.

Cocktail shaker by Stuart, 1934, ht 22.5cm/8¾in, **£800–1,200**

Other engraved glass

In Sweden many designers worked for both of the two major glassworks – Orrefors and Kosta – thus creating a distinctive Scandinavian style based on both careful placing of engraved decoration, and a clever combination of engraved and clear glass to create depth and perspective. The engraving itself fell into two broad styles, both of which are equally collectable: lyrical engraving, incorporating female figures, landscapes, and flora and fauna; and highly stylized and geometric engraving. In the USA the superb quality of glass by Orrefors and Kosta was matched by Steuben Glassworks, where such notable designers as Sidney Waugh and Walter Dorwin Teague produced Art Deco glass with a strong Scandinavian influence.

Vase by Orrefors, from late 1930s, ht 14cm/5½in, **£300–400**

▲ Vase by Orrefors

This mould-blown engraved vase was designed by Sven Palmqvist, one of the leading contemporary Swedish designers. The engraved decoration of a stylized Art Deco maiden with birds has been produced using a deep, broad copper wheel, and the matt finish contrasts with the polished body. Good condition is important with engraved glass, because surface scratches on the engraving plane cannot be polished off. This vase is signed "Orrefors Palmqvist 2397.C.4.A.R.".

▼ Decanter by Orrefors

Vicke Lindstrand, another major Swedish designer, made this hand-blown decanter for Orrefors, although from c.1950 he worked for Kosta. This piece is a typical Art Deco stylized shape, with a stylish black stopper, and linear engraved graphic decoration of a circus scene. It was originally part of a service that also included six trumpet-bowled glasses in different sizes with black feet. Horses, jugglers, and acrobats are all engraved as simple stylized figures with a combination of broad and shallow lines. Marked "OF.L1132", this is a good example of stylish minimalist Swedish design.

Decanter by Orrefors, 1933, ht 30.5cm/11¾in, **£400–500**

Bowl by Kjellander, 1925–31,
ht 11.5cm/4½in, **£120–160**

▲ Bowl by Kjellander

Although not produced
by a major name or factory,
the humour and vitality
of this Swedish bowl make
it highly collectable. The
bowl was thinly blown into
a mould and then engraved
with stylized cross-country
skiers and geometric lines
to create a strong sense
of movement. The piece
bears the signature of
Lars Kjellander, who was
a designer at Kosta from
1881 until 1925, when
he became a freelance
glass-engraver.

Vase by Kjellander, 1925–31,
ht 17cm/6¾in, **£250–350**

▲ Vase by Kjellander

Although this vase, also by
Kjellander, is very different in
style and treatment from the
bowl shown left, the same
sense of movement is found
in it. Here he has used thicker
glass and exploited the
optical effects achievable
by engraving on both sides.
Skilful deep engraving on
such areas as the legs make
the concave surface appear
convex, and the use of random,
soft, flowing abrasions and soft
matt surfaces gives an added
perspective and creates the
impression of the wind blowing.

"Agnus Dei" vase,
c.1935, ht 18.5cm/
7in, **£800–1,200**

▶ "Agnus Dei" vase by Steuben Glassworks

This firm is
known for the
superb quality
of its engraved
glass, of which
this "Agnus Dei"
vase, designed by
Sidney Waugh, is a
fine example. The stylized
matt engraving has a distinctly
American Art Deco feel,
reminiscent of car mascots
and skyscraper decoration.
All Steuben pieces are marked,
sometimes also with the name
of the designer. The value of
this vase reflects its status as
a major piece by a top firm.

Acid-etched glass

Following early Swedish experiments with acid-etching in the late 18thC, in 1857 the British firm of W.H., B. & J. Richardson patented a technique for fine acid-etched work. A gutta-percha resist was applied to the glass, the design was scratched through it, and the glass then exposed to acid, which ate into the unprotected glass. After World War I, British and French glass makers used acid-etching primarily to eat away the background on art glass. Acid-etched pieces by the French firm of Daum Frères are very sought after; prices and desirability depend on size, complexity, and depth of decoration.

Champagne/cocktail glass by Daum, 1930s, ht 12cm/4¾in, **£300–400** (for a pair)

▶ Champagne/cocktail glass by Daum Frères
Acid-etching was a costly technique and was rarely used for tableware. However, it was a popular method of decorating cocktail sets; this hand-blown glass – now one of a pair – was probably one of six. The shallow, acid-etched decoration on the trumpet stem of such high-quality pieces was carried out by hand; on less-exclusive pieces a transfer or template resist might have been used. Drinking glasses are a popular collecting niche, and cocktail glasses in particular have become synonymous with the hedonistic "Jazz" age of the 1920s and 1930s. This glass is signed, as are all pieces by Daum.

▼ Powder box and cover by Daum Frères
The ingenious design of this powder box allows the whole top to be lifted off the smooth, rounded base. The powder is stored in a internal container made of clear, undecorated glass that does not detract from the fine, etched, stylized geometric and floral panels of the cover. This piece, which features some hand-finishing on the hand-blown bowl, was originally part of a dressing-table set that would have been very highly priced in the 1930s. With pieces such as this, if the etched surface was too sharp the piece would be redipped in acid to create a smoother polished finish.

Powder box and cover by Daum, 1930s, ht 10cm/4in, **£400–500**

▼ Vase by Daum Frères

On this thinly blown vase, acid-etching has been combined with other techniques to create an extraordinary variety of textures. The pattern has been randomly etched; the glass has been sandblasted to produce a matt surface, and then randomly hand-polished to create a variety of textures. The iceberg-like effect is heightened by the pale blue colour. The skilful use of techniques and the large size both contribute to the value; smaller wares would be more affordable. Although this piece is marked "Daum", typically no individual designer is credited.

Bowl by Daum, 1930s, ht 10.5cm/4in, **£1,500–2,000**

▲ Bowl by Daum Frères

Pieces as deeply etched as this hand-blown bowl were very costly to make, and are rare and desirable today. Prolonged exposure to acid would have been needed to create the deeply etched background that contrasts with the bright, hand-polished geometric motifs in relief. The Daum mark is clearly visible on the thick, shiny base.

▼ "Iced" cocktail shaker by Orrefors

The cocktail shaker, an essential part of the Art Deco lifestyle, was introduced to the Orrefors range in the 1920s. This piece is part of the "Iced" series that included ashtrays, bowls, and cocktail glasses. The body was cased in blue and blown into an optic mould, and the cockerel design was protected with a resist before the shaker was plunged into a weak acid to create the "iced" effect. Although most of the firm's pieces bear marks, some from the "Iced" series do not; however, they can be identified from Orrefors catalogues.

"Iced" cocktail shaker by Orrefors, ht 23cm/9in, **£150–250**

Vase by Daum, 1930s, ht 23cm/9in, **£700–800**

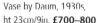

French cameo glass

The cameo technique involves fusing two or more layers of glass in various colours, and then hand-carving, acid-etching, or sandblasting the design so that it stands proud of the background. British supremacy in cameo in the 19thC gave way late in that century to French production, with one of the greatest exponents being Emile Gallé. It is possible that Gallé was inspired by the "Portland" vase, a blue-and-white cameo amphora dating from the 1stC BC to the 1stC AD, in London; Gallé in turn inspired the Nancy-based brothers Auguste and Antonin Daum. Production continued in Gallé's workshop after his death in 1904, and in the 1920s and 1930s most pieces (in line with cameo glass in general) were made on an assembly line, using acid-etching. The variety available to collectors is very wide; the maker, size, number of layers, and complexity of the design will determine desirability.

◀ **Vase by Gallé**
Made by and sold through the Gallé workshop in Nancy, this vase is a fine example of a piece with complex cameo decoration. The pale body has been cased in blue glass, which has been etched away at various levels to create an atmospheric landscape and an extraordinary sense of perspective. This piece is signed "Emile Gallé" in script. All Gallé pieces must be signed, but collectors should beware as there is a proliferation of Gallé fakes on the market, most of which bear marks. The best guarantee of authenticity is to buy from a reputable dealer.

Vase by Gallé,
mid-1920s,
ht 19cm/7in,
£1,500–1,800

▼ **Vase by Gallé**
This vase shows one of the rarer colour combinations of the 1920s, and the design clearly shows the differing shades achievable using the cameo technique. The dark red of the leaves has been given extra texture by the use of lines for the veins; lighter red shading around the outlines of the leaves creates the impression of added relief, and the pink, or half-red, flowers provide colour contrast. Such a vase, signed in relief in cameo on the back, is a good example of middle-range Gallé wares.

Vase by Gallé,
1920s,
ht 9cm/3½in,
£1,000–1,200

▼ Bud vase by Gallé

This bud vase is typical of the many small commercial pieces made by the Gallé workshop. The design is simple compared with the examples shown left, and the colours are more muted, but such an authentic signed Gallé piece is still very desirable. Although muted, the colours on this vase are soft and appealing, whereas those used in reproduction Gallé are harsh approximations. Reproductions made in Eastern Europe should be marked "Tip Gallé"; however, collectors should beware as some unscrupulous vendors remove the "Tip" in order to pass pieces off as originals.

Bud vase by Gallé,
1920s, ht 10.5cm/4in,
£350–450

▼ "Elephant" vase by Gallé

This vase shows the rare "blow-out" technique in which multi-layered casing was blown into a mould with an intaglio design (in this case, elephants). The originals remain exceedingly rare, but a new generation of reproductions have been made, clearly marked "Tip Gallé". Many of these are very modestly priced and allow the collector to have an example, albeit a reproduction, of a piece that would be way beyond the average price range.

"Elephant" vase by Gallé, c.1920,
ht 38.5cm/15in, **£20,000–30,000**

◄ Vase by Daum Frères

The most skilful cameo workers used up to five layers of colour, which demanded great technical expertise because of the different rates at which colours cool. Daum Frères was initially inspired by the Gallé glass exhibited in 1889 in Paris, although most of its landscape cameo vases were produced just after World War I. This superb large example has multiple layers of colour, which adds to its value; the pale blue flowers are enamelled – a popular Daum feature. The mark near the base is typical.

Vase by Daum,
1920s, ht 23cm/9in,
£2,500–3,000

Other cameo glass

The firms of Gallé and Daum Frères were by no means the only French makers creating good production-line cameo. Although their pieces command premium prices and are most sought after, many smaller French factories made cameo glass of equal merit but far more modestly priced today. In Sweden, Kosta developed a distinctive stylized one-colour cameo range that exploited the high quality of the company's glass, and in Britain, Thomas Webb & Sons and H.G. Richardson & Sons also developed popular cameo lines that combined clear glass with a single colour.

▼ Vase by Richard

The quality of the small cameo vases made by the Richard glassworks in Lorraine, such as the piece shown here, is on a par with the later industrial Gallé cameo, but is far more modestly priced. The oriental floral design is typical of the factory, as is the use of two bold colours – three-colour pieces are rare. Signed in cameo script on the back, this vase represents excellent value for money.

Vase by Richard, 1920s, ht 9cm/3in, £150–250

▶ Vase by Stourbridge Glass Co.

Pad cameo was a comparatively rarely used technique that involved applying pads of coloured glass to a flint body. The clear background was then etched and cut away to leave the coloured decoration in higher relief, ready for further carving to provide extra detail. Although unmarked, this vase can be attributed to Stourbridge Glass Co. on the strength of a similar piece, which is marked. Larger, luxury "rock crystal" pad-cameo vases made by Thomas Webb & Sons are worth roughly ten times as much as this little vase.

Vase by Stourbridge, late 1920s, ht 12cm/4in, £400–600

"Rich Cameo" vase by
Webb, mid-1930s, ht
19.5cm/7¾in, **£300–400**

"Cameo Fleur" vase by Webb,
1930s, ht 25cm/9¾in, **£300–400**

▲ "Cameo Fleur" vase by Thomas Webb & Sons

This waisted vase was made in clear glass, overlaid in yellow. The background was then etched away to leave the flowers in relief. Further relief was achieved by cutting, and a final acid polish produced a bright shiny finish. Introduced in 1931, "Cameo Fleur" vases were made in various shapes and colours. The Webb signature appears in the cameo decoration on pieces without feet (such as this vase), or on the top of the foot. Chipped feet can pose a problem, as restoration may bring the signature dangerously near to the edge or even obliterate it.

▲ "Rich Cameo" vase by Thomas Webb & Sons

Thomas Webb & Sons took over the firm of H.G. Richardson in 1930, but pieces in the "Rich Cameo" range still featured the Richardson mark. On vases in the range, the coloured decoration is flat, with indentations for the detailing on the leaves, and the clear flint ground is randomly cut to create a snakeskin-like effect. Vases and bowls were made in "green", "blue", "yellow", "amethyst", and, rarest and most desirable, "red".

"Camé" vase, 1935,
ht 18cm/7in, **£400–500**

▼ "Camé" vase by Kosta

This vase, part of the "Camé" range of one-colour cameo (greens and blues were also used), was probably created by Tyra Lundgren, a Swedish designer who lived in Paris and sent her sketches to Kosta. The thick, horizontal optic-ribbing with random lines creates a watery ground for the angel fish in relief. Such cameo pieces were valuable, exhibition items – an optic-ribbed vase with engraved decoration would be about a quarter of the price of this piece (marked "Kosta 1935" and "Camé 152E").

Enamelled glass

Enamelling was first used by the Ancient Egyptians, Syrians, and Romans, and was hugely popular in the 16thC and 17thC when it was widely used on drinking glasses. The technique involves painting a mixture of metal oxides and powdered glass onto the surface of a piece, which is then fired to fuse the decoration. In the 1920s and 1930s most glassmaking companies in Britain and continental Europe used enamelled freehand or transfer-printed Art Nouveau- and Art Deco-inspired motifs on a wide range of glass. Much sought after are high-quality pieces with decoration by such major designers as Vicke Lindstrand (for Orrefors), members of the Wiener Werkstätte ("Vienna Workshops" – for Lobmeyr), Marcel Goupy, and Auguste-Claude Heiligenstein, who executed many of Goupy's designs for Maison Rouard. More affordable are the stylish tableware pieces produced by a large number of European manufacturers.

Vase by Argy-Rousseau, 1930s, ht 15.5cm/6in, £1,500–2,000

◀ **Vase by Argy-Rousseau**
Although primarily known for his *pâte-de-verre* glass (*see* pp.30–31), from the mid-1930s Gabriel Argy-Rousseau made a series of rare enamelled vases. This blown smoky grey/brown vase has an Egyptian-style frieze of enamelled elephants walking along a stylized black path – wild animals were a popular Art Deco motif; the style may well reflect Argy-Rousseau's passion for photography. Such a rare, signed vase will be much sought after.

▼ **Footed bowl by Luce**
Jean Luce was the son of a Parisian tableware retailer. In 1931 he opened his own shop, specializing in ceramics and glass. He was a designer rather than maker of glass, and his early designs of the 1920s included enamelled decoration, such as the Cubist-inspired geometric floral design shown here, signed with an enamelled "JL". Such early enamelled pieces are quite rare, as Luce later abandoned the technique as "too bright", concentrating instead on engraving and etching.

Footed bowl by Luce, 1920s, ht 26cm/10¼in, £1,800–2,200

▼ Goblet by Vedart

This unsigned goblet is one of a series thought to have been produced as promotional material by the Venetian glassworks Vedart (short for "Vetri d'Arte"). The goblets were produced in sets of six and in two designs: one decorated with a band of *putti* and the other, more sought after and valuable, the fabulous lady and peacock design shown here. The form of the goblets, which were blown in one size only, is unremarkable; their appeal lies in the superb enamelled decoration, which is beautifully shown off in the peacock's tail.

Goblet by Vedart, 1930s, ht 19.5cm/7½in, £400–500 (with peacocks), £300–400 (with *putti*)

▼ Vase by Vedart

Vedart may well have been a decorating company that bought in glass blanks from other factories, as this vase is another example of a rather mundane form transformed by wonderful, polychrome, freehand-enamelled decoration. Here the influence is fashionably oriental, with handpainted branches, blossoms, and insects, and the Vedart signature in enamel. Good condition of the decoration is essential—any damage will drastically reduce the value, as it is impossible to restore enamelling successfully.

Vase by Vedart, 1920s, ht 22cm/8in, £1,000–1,500

- A combination of good form and good decoration is most desirable, but some everyday forms can be transformed by top-quality polychrome enamelled decoration.
- Decoration must be in tip-top condition. Badly abraded enamelling will look like a foxed print and should be avoided.
- Pieces with enamelled decoration must be treated gently, and cleaned with soft cloths.
- Both handpainted and transfer designs were used; the latter are usually more affordable.

▼ Vase

This unsigned, cut and enamelled vase was sold through a Paris retailer and is therefore assumed to be French, although it may well have been made elsewhere. Mould-blown, it has vertical sliced cuts and alternate panels transferred with black enamel designs. It is rather large and unusual; cocktail sets of decanters and four matching glasses in the same style are more commonly found.

Vase, 1930s, ht 18cm/7in, £400–500

Perfume bottle atomizer, late 1920s/early 1930s, ht 12cm/4¾in, **£150–200**

Vase by Webb Corbett, 1930s, ht 25cm/10in, **£200–300**

▲ Perfume bottle atomizer

Small and easy to display, perfume bottles form a popular collecting niche that epitomizes the glamour of the Art Deco period. This mould-blown bottle has a transfer band of enamelled roses *en grisaille* (grey), and may well have been a promotional bottle for a rose scent. Although bottles without the atomizer workings are readily found and very inexpensive, they are best avoided, as restoration will be both costly and extremely difficult to carry out successfully.

▲ Vase by Webb Corbett Ltd

Increasing interest is being shown in Webb Corbett glass since a recent exhibition of the company's cut-and-engraved, etched, and enamelled pieces, and prices are likely to rise as a result. The blown, footed vase featured above unusually combines acid-etched decoration of stylized pendant motifs with translucent black and blue enamels. The vase, which bears the mark used by the firm in the 1930s, was probably very highly priced at that time, owing to the complexity of the enamelling technique.

▼ Vase by Stuart & Sons

Enamelling could be either painted freehand onto a piece or applied using a combination of transfer-printing (for the outline) and hand-painting, as in the case of the stylized pendant flowers on this large blown vase. This type of glass design, which combined enamelling and glass trailing, was introduced by Stuart & Sons in 1931 and produced in various shapes, sizes and designs. The large size and typical Deco colour combination make this vase, marked "Stuart England", particularly attractive.

Vase by Stuart, 1930s, ht 31cm/12in, **£300–350**

▼ Candlestick by Stuart & Sons

The enamelled decoration on this free blown candlestick is an unusual example of typical Deco colours and geometric motifs applied to British glass tableware. It is possible that the freehand-painted design was influenced by the phenomenally successful handpainted ceramics designed by Clarice Cliff, and as such the candlestick is very collectable as a single piece in general, they are much more valuable as pairs. Marked "Stuart Made in England", this candlestick represents the company's middle-range wares – between the vase shown left and the mass market tableware exemplified by the bowl shown right.

▼ Bowl by Stuart & Sons

The mould-blown bowl featured below, which was available both plain and with patterned decoration, is part of a table service that was one of Stuart's flagship inexpensive, cheerful, modern designer wares. The first coloured enamelled patterns were introduced by Stuart in 1927, and by 1929 over a third of all new patterns produced by the firm were enamelled. This design, by Ludwig Kny (see pp.32–3), was one of the most commonly found. The bowl is marked "Stuart England", together with the number "RD 681309", which refers to the shape rather than the pattern.

FACT FILE

• Cocktail sets and vases in stylish Deco patterns tend to be found in two qualities: fine examples in heavy lead glass, with a fine, bright finish, and mass-produced versions (many made in Czechoslovakia – now the Czech Republic) in lighter, thinner glass, typically with a slightly yellow tinge.

• Pieces by less well known factories are often underrated and undervalued; increasing interest in British Art Deco glass may bring such firms into the front line of collecting, with a corresponding increase in prices.

• Any piece by a less well-known factory or designer must be in perfect condition for top value.

• An unusual mix of enamelling with another decorative technique will increase value.

Bowl by Stuart, 1930s, diam. 20cm/7¾in, £50–70

Candlestick by Stuart, 1930s, ht 8cm/3in, £60–90 (£150–200 for a pair)

Table glass

In the 1920s and 1930s, Art Deco table-glass production was dominated by Scandinavian glassmakers, particularly those in Sweden. Their distinctive, timeless interpretation of the style, combined with high-quality production, makes such pieces highly attractive to collectors, who can, with patience, build up complete sets. In Britain a few manufacturers produced Art Deco table services; the majority remained committed both to the reproduction Irish-style glass that was popular in the USA and to table services in a Neo-Georgian style. Similarly, most Italian glassmakers produced historical rather than Art Deco table glass. Collectors have a choice of two distinct styles, and can also choose whether to build up complete table services or collect interesting examples of individual pieces.

▼ Celery vase

By the late 19thC celery had become such a popular food that many makers produced vases engraved with the word "celery", intended specifically to hold celery sticks. "Celery vase" is now used to describe all footed, short-stemmed, tall, narrow vases made from c.1800. This affordable example is a press-moulded, unsigned piece that can be dated to the 1930s by its Deco design, and is a good starting-point for novice collectors.

Celery vase, 1930s, ht 23.5cm/9in, £20–30

▶ Incorporator bottle by Gill

Incorporator bottles, such as the example by Stan Gill shown right, were used for making vinaigrette. The internal ridges that appear externally as silver decorative bands help the liquid swirl down the bottle, and are a development from the bottles in the shape of the "Michelin Man" that were popular in the Victorian period. The blown stopper on this piece appears cloudy owing to condensation. Usually this would detract from the value, but the rarity, technical skill, and ingenuity of this example, and the affection and esteem in which Gill was held in his native Stourbridge, ensure that it retains its value.

Incorporator bottle by Gill, 1930s, ht 21cm/8in, £80–120

"Harlequin" hock glass by Walsh, 1930s, ht 20cm/7¾in, £25–30

• Drinking glasses are among the most easily found, modestly priced items of glass tableware. Complete sets of six glasses are rare, but individual pieces are collectable on their own.
• Be wary of hock glasses with coloured, cased bowls, geometric cutting, and clear stems, unless they are dated and attributable to a specific maker, as there are many modern copies.

Double-ended champagne glass, 1930s, ht 22cm/8½in, £80–120

▲ "Harlequin" hock glass by John Walsh Walsh

This "citron" glass is one of a "Harlequin" set that would have included five other glasses – one each of "green", "pale blue", "dark blue", "ruby", and "amethyst". Walsh glasses were mainly geometrically cut, as shown here, although this example actually bears a fake Webb mark, which was probably added in the 1970s when glass by Thomas Webb & Sons was avidly collected. Unfortunately, this piece also has an area of yellow colour missing, where the glass has not been properly dipped.

▲ Double-ended champagne glass

The 1930s debate as to whether champagne should be served in a flute or a saucer was solved by this double-ended champagne glass, which has a slightly iridized finish. It was made in Austria, where such pieces were also known as "marriage" glasses or "wedding" goblets, and came in many intricate designs. Gilt and enamelling were common before World War I, but in the 1930s the designs were more subtle. The flat cutting across the tops and bottoms makes them slightly rough to drink from, but they are great fun to collect. Although initially made in sets, these glasses are now mostly found as single items.

Ice bucket, 1930s, ht 13.5cm/5¼in, £60–80 (for a pair without liners) or £120–140 (for a pair with liners)

▲ Ice bucket

This piece, probably originally one of a pair, was mould-blown, and the "icy" surface decoration was created by fusing crushed glass to the outside surface. Indentations about a third of the way up from the base were designed to hold a metal fretwork liner (often missing), which allowed water from the melting ice to drip through.

Decanter by Stevens & Williams, c.1934, ht 24.5cm/9½in, **£100–150** (unmarked), **£250–300** (marked), **£600–800** (for a pair)

Teapot by Schott, 1930s, ht 17cm/6¾in, **£200–240**

▲ Teapot by Schott

The influence of the Modern Movement can be clearly seen in this glass teapot, which was made in two shapes – the other version was slightly more angular. It was one of the first examples of the lampwork technique being used to produce scientific glass in a design context. A classic example of Bauhaus-inspired glass, this teapot may have been designed by Wilhelm Wagenfeld, who worked for Schott from 1931 until 1935, designing a range of heat-resistant glass household containers that have become 20thC design classics. The example above is marked "Schott Mainz Jena Glass".

Candlestick, 1930s, ht 15cm/6in, **£50–70** (**£200–300** for a pair)

▲ Candlestick

Made of thin soda glass, with a large folded foot, this candlestick (originally one of a pair) is a good example of the historical designs favoured by Italian glassmakers in the 1920s and 1930s. Its wrythen hollow stem and applied handles are clearly inspired by early Venetian glass. Such delicate candlesticks are rare: they often cracked when the candles burnt down into the glass cups, and were also very vulnerable to knocks. Collectors should check carefully for damage, especially to prominent handles.

▲ Decanter by Stevens & Williams

Not all Keith Murray's designs for Stevens & Williams were as innovative as his "Cactus" decanter (see pp.38–9). The piece shown above has a very simple form and rather standard decorative band of matt circles, although the black stopper is quintessentially Deco. This piece was part of a complete table service, and appears with a footed tumbler as design 429A in the catalogue of Murray patterns. Marked and unmarked examples are known; the latter can be very affordable, as they will only be attributable by reference to archive material, but if one can be matched with a marked decanter, its value will dramatically increase.

▼ Decanter by Orrefors

The simple, elegant design of this blown decanter, with its wrythen stopper and terraced foot, is typical of Scandinavian tableware. This piece was made by Orrefors in the late 1920s, and can be distinguished from similar designs by the British Whitefriars Glassworks by the colour (the blue on pieces by Whitefriars is softer) and the terraced foot. Plates, bowls, wine glasses, tumblers, and serving dishes were also produced, and with patience it is possible to build up a complete table service.

▼ Console set by Sinclair Glass Co.

This major American firm is best known for its large, high-quality brilliant-cut glass in Victorian style, and the blown console set shown below, in opaque black-and-white glass with engraved and acid-etched decoration, is a rare example of one of its Art Deco pieces. Such console sets as this are very rarely found complete. On its own, the bowl would be worth about £1,000; pairs of candlesticks are worth three or four times as much as single sticks, and sets of four are even more valuable than pairs.

- With decanters, good condition is essential. Check carefully for internal cracks by holding the piece up to the light — especially important with any engraved examples.
- Stoppers should fit snugly; check that they are not stuck. Bad chips on the peg can be polished out, as can "fritting" (tiny chips).
- Cloudiness, which is caused by condensation, and internal limescale deposit, can also be detected by holding the (empty, dry, and clean) decanter up to the light.

Decanter by Orrefors, 1920s, ht 30.5cm/12in, **£80–120**

Console set by Sinclair, c.1920–23, diam. of bowl 45cm/17½in, ht of candlestick 34cm/13¼in, from **£4,000**

Novelties

The fun-loving 1920s and 1930s were frivolous times. There was a vogue for small glass ornaments, and all the major glass manufacturers developed their own novelty lines. Glass animals were ubiquitous; Austrian, Venetian, and American factories were known for their production of glass flowers, and the Austrian firm of Bimini in Vienna was well known for its lampwork and figural pieces, including some examples featuring nubile female forms. Novelty glass is a collecting niche, where bad taste is better than no taste at all, and the worst possible taste may well prove an excellent investment.

▼ Hunting goblet by Stevens & Williams

Hunting goblets were usually produced in sets of six, in a choice of three sizes. The example shown here, made by Stevens & Williams, was one of a set of designs that all featured a small figure in the hollow blown stem. The figures were made by Bill Swingewood, who was known for his highly skilled lampwork. Engraved hunting goblets are rarer and more highly priced than plain ones, but most goblets are good value for money, considering the skill needed to produce them.

Hunting goblet by Stevens & Williams, 1930s, ht 17cm/6¾in, **£100–120**

▶ "Weasel" vase by Ferro Toso & Co.

Novelty glass animals were made in prolific quantities by Italian glassmakers. This impressive vase was designed by Guido Balsamo Stella for Ferro Toso & Co., one of the many glassworks based on the island of Murano, near Venice. Known for its Venetian-style vases and goblets, in the late 1920s the company made a range of novelty ornaments in a more typically Art Deco style. This vase, which is made from tiny pieces of blown glass, would have been very difficult to produce and is vulnerable. Such items were usually marked with a paper label (often missing).

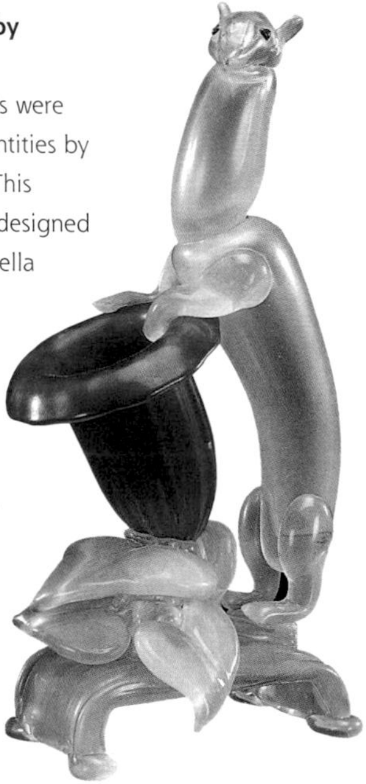

"Weasel" vase by Ferro Toso, c.1930, ht 27cm/10½in, **£2,000–3,000**

▼ Ashtray by Thomas Webb & Sons

The Art Deco vogue for travel and glamour is summed up in this handmade ashtray by the Stourbridge-based firm of Thomas Webb & Sons. Made of separate pieces that were assembled when hot, such ashtrays were highly labour-intensive and very vulnerable. The few that have survived must be in tip-top condition for maximum value. This piece is unsigned, but has been identified from company catalogues.

Ashtray by Webb, 1920s, ht 20cm/8in, **£100–150**

Napkin rings by Davidson, 1937, ht 4cm/1½in, **£100–200**

▲ Napkin rings by George Davidson & Co. Ltd

These mould-blown, hand-finished, cut-glass napkin rings, still with their original fake shagreen presentation box, were made as commemorative souvenirs for the coronation of George VI in 1937. George Davidson & Co. Ltd was a major British glassmaker and these napkin rings were probably fairly highly priced in 1937. What is perhaps lacking in aesthetic appeal is more than compensated for by the presence of original packaging (bearing the original silver label, marked "Davidson's Glassware, London, Made in England"), and the commemorative memorabilia interest.

- Novelties are a popular collecting niche; charm, humour, and ingenious design determine collectability.
- Glass animals are particularly popular, but are rare as they are very vulnerable.
- Baskets are also popular among collectors.
- Perfect condition is important: check vulnerable details carefully for damage and restoration.

▼ "Verre de soie" basket by Steuben Glassworks

"Verre de soie" was the name used by this American firm for its range of clear glass with a silvery iridescence. The silky sheen made the range very popular and led to a long production run (1905–30). The applied handles on this basket shape (designed by Frederick Carder) are fragile, and the crack at the join is visible. A concealed crack can be detected by gently tapping the glass – a good piece will ring, whereas a cracked example will give a dead sound.

"Verre de soie" basket by Steuben, c.1930, ht 43.5cm/17in, **£800–1,200**

Designers, glass makers, & marks

Much art glass made during the 1920s and 1930s is marked. However, some marks can be problematic, either because they are indistinct and difficult to identify, or because they were in the form of a paper label (usually missing). Check the base first, as the mark is often in the centre of the bottom of the piece or on the outside edge of the foot. With cameo and enamelled glass the mark may be an integral part of the main body. If the mark is not obvious, hold the piece up to the light and turn it in various directions; a soft acid signature often shows up when the glass is held against a piece of black cloth or card. Unmarked pieces have to be identified from company archives.

BRITAIN

Bagley & Co. Ltd
(est. Knottingley, Yorkshire, 1871). Some glass impressed with date code.

George Davidson & Co. Ltd
(est. Gateshead-on-Tyne, 1867).

Edinburgh & Leith Flint Glass Co.
(est. Leith, c.1864; acquired by Webb's Crystal Glass Co. 1919).

Gray-Stan Glass
(est. London, 1926; closed 1936). Roughly engraved script signature.

Harbridge Crystal Co. Ltd
(est. Stourbridge, 1928). Acid-etched signature "HARBRIDGE".

James A. Jobling & Co. Ltd
(est. Sunderland, 1885; from 1921 Jobling & Co; taken over 1975). Opalescent art glass impressed with registered design number.

John Moncrieff Ltd ("Monart")
(est. Perth, Scotland, 1865). Paper labels such as the one shown below used 1925 to 1930.

Paper labels such as the one shown below used from 1930 to 1961.

Nazeing Glassworks
(est. London, 1928). Unmarked; identified by known retailers' labels.

James Powell & Sons Ltd
(est. London, 1834; from 1962 Whitefriars Glassworks; closed 1980). No marks or signatures; very occasionally original paper labels; identify items from archives.

H.G. Richardson & Sons
(est. Stourbridge, c.1850; taken over c.1930 by Thomas Webb & Sons). Acid-etched mark of "Richardsons Rich Cameo".

Stevens & Williams
(est. Stourbridge, 1847; from 1930s known as "Royal Brierley"). Wares by Murray for the firm marked from 1934 to 1939 as below.

Stourbridge Glass Co.
(est. Stourbridge, 1922; from 1929 known as Tudor Crystal).

Stuart & Sons Ltd
(est. Stourbridge, 1881). Wares marked as shown below from c.1926 to 1950.

$$Stuart$$
ENGLAND

Mark below used from c.1930 to 1950.

Stuart
ENGLAND

John Walsh Walsh
(est. Birmingham, 1851; closed c.1951). Often not marked; occasionally acid-etched "WALSH" or "WALSH" over "ENGLAND".

Thomas Webb & Sons
(est. Stourbridge, 1859). Mark shown below used c.1906 to 1935.

Webb

Mark below used in the 1930s.

Mark below used c.1935 to 1949.

Webb Corbett Ltd
(est. Stourbridge, 1897 as Thomas Webb & Corbett Ltd; from 1930s Webb Corbett Ltd).
This mark used c.1930 to 1947.

Whitefriars Glassworks
(see James Powell & Sons Ltd).

CONTINENTAL EUROPE

Argy-Rousseau, Gabriel
(1885–1953).
Marked with a signature in shallow relief.

Baccarat
(est. Baccarat, near Lunéville, 1764).
Many pieces unmarked, as original paper labels are missing; some marked "BACCARAT" in script.

Daum Frères
(est. Nancy, France, 1895).
Mark below wheel-cut on foot rim.

Décorchemont, François-Emile
(1880–1971).

Gallé, Emile (1846–1904)
(Cristalleries d'Emile Gallé, est. Nancy, 1867)
Multiplicity of different marks – refer to specialist books.

Kosta
(est. Smaland, Sweden, 1742).
Cameo pieces engraved "Kosta" on base; designer's name and model number sometimes also included.

Lalique, René (1860–1945).
Various signatures used; all include an "R".

Leerdam
(est. Leerdam, near Rotterdam, 1765; still operating).
Pieces often unsigned and original factory label missing.

Loetz (Johann Loetz-Witwe)
(est. Klostermühle, 1840; closed 1939).
Most pieces unsigned; engraved mark used from 1898.

Luce, Jean (1895–1964).

Marinot, Maurice (1882–1960).
Surname incised in script on base.

Navarre, Henri (1885–1971).
Pieces finely diamond-point engraved "H. NAVARRE" on base.

Orrefors
(est. Orrefors, Sweden, 1898).
Engraved signature "Orrefors"; often includes full name or initials of the designer.

Sabino, Marius-Ernest
(1878–1961; glassworks est. Paris, 1920s).

Schneider, Cristalleries
(est. Epinay-sur-Seine, 1913).
Vases usually signed "Schneider" in script or block capitals.

Val-Saint-Lambert Glasshouse
(est. Seraing-sur-Meuse, near Liège, 1825).
Several marks used, often incorporating star-cut design.

Württemberg Metalwork Factory ("WMF")
(est. Geislingen, 1853; glassworks est. Goppingen, 1883).
Mark including the initials "WMF" used from 1914.

Walter, Alméric (1859–1942).
Pieces often signed "A WALTER NANCY".

USA

Steuben Glassworks
(est. New York, 1903, by Frederick Carder; acquired by Corning Glassworks, 1918).

Tiffany, Louis Comfort
(1848–1933)
(Tiffany Glass & Decorating Co. est. Corona, Queens, New York, 1892; closed 1900, Tiffany Studios, est. New York City, 1900).
Tiffany name (signature or initials) and model number typical.

Glossary

acid-etching technique for decorating or reducing ground by using acid to eat away areas unprotected by an acid-resist

acid-polishing process used to give a shiny finish by dipping glass into a mixture of hydrofluoric and sulphuric acid

aventurine from the Italian word for "chance"; decoration of flecked metallic particles

batch the mixture of molten glass in the pot

blowing iron long, hollow metal rod used to inflate the gather of glass

cameo cased glass, with two or more coloured layers, with the background carved or acid-etched away to create relief decoration

canes rods of glass drawn by the glass-blower to required thickness for use as decoration

cased pieces made of two or more layers of coloured glass or with coloured decoration sandwiched between two layers of clear glass

cutting deep cuts, either polished or matt, created by offering the piece to a stone wheel at various angles

diamond-point engraving minutely detailed, fine line decoration using a stiletto-type tool with a sharp diamond point

enamelling decorative technique in which coloured powdered glass suspended in an oily mixture is painted onto a piece and then fused by heating

engraving lightly abraded matt surface decoration created with a fine copper wheel

flint clear lead or soda glass

gather molten glass on the end of a blowing or pontil iron

hand-blown free-blown glass whose shape is entirely formed through blowing and finishing on the pontil rod

iridescence rainbow-like surface effect created with lustre colours or by exposing piece to hot vapours of metal oxides

lampwork glass made from clear or coloured rods worked over a blow lamp or torch

lead glass heavy, brilliant glass with a high lead content; rings when struck

"lost-wax" casting technique in which a wax model is cased in plaster and the wax then steamed out ("lost") to make a mould for *pâte-de-cristal* and *pâte-de-verre*; also known as *cire perdue*

lustres metal oxides suspended in an oily material and used for painting onto hot glass

marver metal table used for rolling glass into shape

mitre cutting very deep, V-shaped cuts

mould-blowing method of blowing molten glass into a mould to produce both shape and pattern

optic decoration within or on the surface of the glass, which reflects the light in patterns

pâte-de-cristal ("crystal paste") translucent ware made from finely powdered glass paste using "lost-wax" casting

pâte-de-verre ("glass paste") opaque pieces made from crushed glass by the "lost-wax" casting technique

pontil iron solid iron rod used to transfer the blown bubble of glass from the blowing iron for further shaping and/or finishing

pontil mark scar where the pontil iron or rod was removed from the base of a piece

pot crucible in which glass is melted

pressed glass glass with a smooth interior and a moulded exterior made by being pressed into a mould by a plunger

prunt blob of glass, in various shapes, applied as decoration

refraction deflection of rays of light from a glass surface

satin glass also known as *verre de soie*; glass with a satin finish

soda glass light, malleable glass with a slightly brownish or greenish tinge; has no lead content and does not ring when struck

star cutting multiple cuts meeting at a central point to create a star effect

studio glass one-off pieces designed and produced by artist-craftsmen

trailing thin threads of glass applied to the surface of a piece

transfer-printing design printed on paper from an engraved copper plate and applied to the surface of a piece

Waldglas ("Forest glass") type of greenish-yellowish glass originally produced in Germany in the Middle Ages

wrythen spiral-twisted ribbed glass

Where to buy

For the new collector, the best place to start buying glass is from a specialist dealer who is a member of one of the antiques associations: LAPADA (the Association of Art and Antique Dealers) and/or BADA (the British Antique Dealers' Association). Most dealers are only too pleased to share their knowledge and experience, provide an opportunity to handle glass, and, most importantly, provide a descriptive receipt. Vetted fairs are also good places to start, and the major annual fairs are held at the venues given below. Markets and car boot sales are usually best avoided until you have sufficient expertise to distinguish between the masses of glass on show. Similarly, it is probably best only to buy from auction houses once you are more familiar with the area and market values. Although no substitute for actually handling glass, museums offer an opportunity to look at and learn about major glass collections; those listed all have collections that will broaden your visual experience and add to your historical knowledge.

SPECIALIST DEALERS

Alfies Antiques Market
13–25 Church Street
Marylebone
London NW8 8DT

Artemis
36 Kensington Church Street
London W8 4BX

Nigel Benson
58–60 Kensington Church Street
London W8 4DB

Antiques Centre
Camden Passage
Upper Street
London N1 8ED

**The Ginnell Gallery
Antiques Centre**
18–22 Lloyd Street
Manchester M2 5WA

Jeanette Hayhurst
Kensington Church Street
London W8 4HA

**Kensington Church Street
Antiques Centre**
58–60 Kensington Church Street
London W8 4DB

ANTIQUES FAIRS

**British International
Antiques Fair**
National Exhibition Centre
Birmingham B40 1NS
(April/August)

Fine Art & Antiques Fair
Olympia
Hammersmith Road
London W14 8UX
(February/June)

MAJOR AUCTION HOUSES

Bonhams (Chelsea)
65–69 Lots Road
London SW10 0RN

Christie's South Kensington
85 Old Brompton Road
London SW7 3LD

Phillips
101 New Bond Street
London W1Y 0AS

Sotheby's
34–35 New Bond Street
London W1A 2AA

MUSEUMS

**Broadfield House
Glass Museum**
Compton Drive
Kingswinford
West Midlands DY6 9NS

**Cecil Higgins Art Gallery
and Museum**
Castle Close
Bedford MK10 3NY

Manchester City Art Gallery
Moseley Street
Manchester M2 3JL

Victoria and Albert Museum
Cromwell Road
London SW7 2RL

What to read

There are many excellent books on glass of this period. The list below gives a selection of general and more specialist books, all of which should be available from either good bookshops or libraries.

GENERAL BOOKS

Arwas, V. Glass: Art Nouveau to Art Deco (London, 1977)

Beard, G. International Modern Glass (London, 1976)

Cummings, K. Techniques of Kiln-Formed Glass (London, 1997)

Dodsworth, R., ed. British Glass Between the Wars (Kingswinford, 1987)

Drahotova, O. European Glass (Prague, 1983)

Janneau, G. Modern Glass (Stourbridge, 1931)

Ploak, A. Modern Glass (London, 1962)

Stennett-Wilson, R. Modern Glass (London, 1975)

SPECIALIST BOOKS

Andrews, F., Clarke, A., and Turner, I. Ysart Glass (London, 1990)

Bacri, Clotilde Daum: Masters of French Decorative Glass (London, 1993)

Baldwin, G.D. Moser Artistic Glass (Ohio, 1997)

Barovier, M. and Doigato, A., eds Animals in Glass (Venice, 1996)

Barovier Mentasti, Rosa Venetian Glass 1890–1980 (Venice, 1992)

Bloch-Dermant, J.G. Argy-Rousseau: Glassware as Art (London, 1991)

Corning Museum of Glass Czechoslovakian Glass 1350–1980 (New York, 1981)

Deboni, F. and Klein, D. Venini Glass (Verona, c.1996)

Duncan, A. Orrefors Glass (Woodbridge, 1995)

Duncan, A. and De Bartha, G. Glass by Gallé (London, 1984)

Evans, W., Ross, C., and Werner, A. Whitefriars Glass: James Powell & Sons of London (London, 1985)

Forsythe, R.A. Made in Czechoslovakia (Ohio, 1982)

Gardner, P.V. Frederick Carder: Portrait of a Glassmaker (New York, 1985)

Jackson, L., ed. Whitefriars Glass: The Art of James Powell & Sons (Shepton Beauchamp, 1996)

Opie, J. Scandinavian Ceramics and Glass in the 20th Century (London, 1989)

Osteergard, D. and Strizler-Levine, N., eds The Brilliance of Swedish Glass 1918–1939 (Yale, 1996)

Petrova, S. and Olvie, J.-L. Bohemian Glass 1400–1989 (New York, 1990)

Ricke, H. and T., eds Swedish Glass Factories, Production Catalogues 1915–1960 (Munich, 1987)

Index

Acknowledgements
All pictures photgraphed by Premier Photography for Octopus Publishing Group Ltd, courtesy of Jeanette Hayhurst, except:
31tc Christie's Images; **13tc, 31br, 41r, 55br, 57br** Corning Museum of Glass; **23tc, 23br** Haworth Art Gallery, Accrington; **7, 8r, 15tc, 15br, 21tc, 21br, 24r, 26l, 26r, 33bc, 34tl, 39br, 46tr, 47tl, 47tc, 50tc, 50br, 51bl, 57bl** Jeanette Hayhurst; **35bl** Mallett, 141 New Bond Street, London W1Y 0BS; **37tc** Octopus Publishing Group Ltd/Tim Ridley/Namdar Antiques, B22 Grays Mews Antique Market, 1–7 Davies Mews, London W1Y 1AR; **49br** Octopus Publishing Group Ltd/Tim Ridley/Tagore Ltd, stand 302, Grays Antique Market, 58 Davies Street, London W1Y 2LP; **50tl** Octopus Publishing Group Ltd/Tim Ridley/Trio, stand L24, Grays Mews Antiques Market, 1–7 Davies Mews, London W1Y 2LP; **12l, 12r, 13bl, 20r, 30l, 30r, 31l, 45bc, 48l, 48r, 56r** Sotheby's Picture Library; **2** Octopus Publishing Group Ltd/Steve Tanner/Jeanette Hayhurst.
Jacket photograph Octopus Publishing Group Ltd/Steve Tanner/Jeanette Hayhurst.